CANAL HOUSE
COOKING

D1227776

CANAL HOUSE
No. 6 Coryell Street
Lambertville, NJ 08530
thecanalhouse.com

ISBN 978-0-615-31830-1

Printed in China

Book design by CANAL HOUSE, a group of artists who collaborate on design projects.
This book was designed by Melissa Hamilton, Christopher Hirsheimer & Teresa Hopkins.
Authors' photo by Teresa Hopkins.
Edited by Margo True.
Copyedited by Valerie Saint-Rossy.

Distributed to the trade by
Andrews McMeel Publishing, LLC
an Andrews McMeel Universal company
1130 Walnut Street, Kansas City, Missouri 64106

www.andrewsmcmeel.com

11 12 13 14 OGP 10 9 8 7 6 5 4 3

ATTENTION: SCHOOLS AND BUSINESSES
Andrews McMeel books are available at quantity discounts with bulk purchase for
educational, business, or sales promotional use. For information, please e-mail
the Andrews McMeel Publishing Special Sales Department:
specialsales@amuniversal.com

CANAL HOUSE
COOKING

Volume N° 2

Hamilton & Hirsheimer

Christopher and Melissa in the Canal House kitchen

Welcome to Canal House—our studio, workshop, dining room, office, kitchen, and atelier devoted to good ideas and good work relating to the world of food. We write, photograph, design, and paint, but in our hearts we both think of ourselves as cooks first.

Our loft studio is in an old redbrick warehouse. A beautiful lazy canal runs alongside the building. We have a simple galley kitchen. Two small apartment-size stoves sit snugly side by side against a white tiled wall. We have a dishwasher, but prefer to hand wash the dishes so we can look out of the tall window next to the sink and see the ducks swimming in the canal or watch the raindrops splashing into the water.

And every day we cook. Starting in the morning we tell each other what we made for dinner the night before. Midday, we stop our work, set the table simply with paper napkins, and have lunch. We cook seasonally because that's what makes sense. So it came naturally to write down what we cook. The recipes in our books are what we make for ourselves and our families all year long. If you cook your way through a few, you'll see that who we are comes right through in the pages: that we are crazy for tomatoes in summer, make braises and stews all fall, and turn oranges into marmalade in winter.

Canal House Cooking is home cooking by home cooks for home cooks. We use ingredients found in most markets. All the recipes are easy to prepare for the novice and experienced cook alike. We want to share them with you as fellow cooks along with our love of food and all its rituals. The everyday practice of simple cooking and the enjoyment of eating are two of the greatest pleasures in life.

CHRISTOPHER HIRSHEIMER served as food and design editor for *Metropolitan Home* magazine, and was one of the founders of *Saveur* magazine, where she was executive editor. She is a writer and a photographer.

MELISSA HAMILTON cofounded the restaurant Hamilton's Grill Room in Lambertville, New Jersey, where she served as executive chef. She worked at *Martha Stewart Living*, *Cook's Illustrated*, and at *Saveur* as the food editor.

 Fall

It's Always Five O'Clock Somewhere
getting drunk by colman andrews 8
negroni 10, a straight negroni 10, jack manhattan 10

Working up an Appetite
fried zucchini 15, beans with sausage and tuna 18
mushrooms on toast 19, mushroom ragù on polenta 20

Eat Your Vegetables
braised endive 25, fennel gratin 25, beets with butter and tarragon 26
mashed rutabagas with loads of scallions 26
roasted red peppers with currants and capers 28

Down & Dirty
pommes anna 32, potatoes anna 32, rösti 35
sister frances' potatoes 35

Long & Slow
serious ragù 38, beef with carrots 41
lamb shoulder cooked in red wine 42, breast of veal braised with chiles 44

If It Looks Like, Walks Like, Quacks Like…
roast duck and potatoes 49, the love token 50
duck with turnips and rice 50, duck with apples and onions 53
poached duck eggs on bitter greens 55

Pears, Apples & Chocolate
pear sorbet 58, apple pie 62, chocolate gingerbread 63

Holiday Baking
currant gingersnaps 66, shortbread 67, pain d'épice 68, golden fruitcake 69

The Holidays

THANKSGIVING

hot spiked cider 74, french cheese puffs 74, shrimp and pickled celery 75
pumpkin soup with pimentón and preserved lemon 78
triple x chicken broth with ricotta ravioli 79
neenie's sourdough-sage stuffing 80, chestnut stuffing 81
roast capon with fettuccine stuffing 82, roast turkey 84
glazed carrots 85, brian's mashed potato trick 85, creamed onions 85
cranberry port gelée 86, ode to cranberry sauce 86
sweet potato pie 90, agee's pecan pie 91

LA VIGILIA—CHRISTMAS EVE

whole fish baked on potatoes 95
white asparagus with anchovy vinaigrette 97, broiled mussels 97
poached oysters with lemon 97, lobster stew 98
brandade 100, langoustine lace 100

CHRISTMAS DINNERS

hot toddy 103, milk punch 103, the fisherman's wife's gravlax 105
roast prime rib of beef 106, little yorkshire puddings 106
crown roast of pork with corn bread stuffing 110
baked apples with savory stuffing 111, parsnip purée 113
bûche de noël 114

HAPPY NEW YEAR

roger sherman's blini 122, cheese straws 122
coq au vin 124, watercress salad 125
grand marnier soufflé 129

HAIR OF THE DOG BRUNCH

ramos fizz 130, bitter greens with sweet grapefruit 130, eggs en cocotte 132

Welcome to Canal House

Some people find it sad to see summer go, but as the air cools and the light turns golden, our appetites build—we're hungry to eat and ready to cook. At Canal House, fall starts the season for some serious home cooking.

The autumnal sun rises later each morning. And now, whichever one of us arrives at our studio first switches on all the lights, builds a fire in the old wood stove, and starts the espresso machine. Everything begins to look cozy and cheery.

Early in the season we start a fall cleanup. We pull on our pink rubber gloves and tear the stove apart, cleaning every crevice in the oven: it will get a good workout from October until after the new year. We take inventory of our little pantry; we'll need to fill the canisters with flour and sugar and stock the shelves with currants and prunes, cinnamon sticks and anise seeds, vanilla beans and almond extract. The fruit from Melissa's pear tree is packed in boxes and stored in her garage—we'll make pear sorbet in November. The wooden box that holds all our holiday baking recipes comes down from the shelf, and we begin to make lists.

The markets are bearing big time. So we put on our sweaters and jump in the car to check out the late harvest bounty. The apple trees in Amy and Gary's orchard are heavy with Honey Crisps and Ginger Golds—two of our favorites for making apple pie. We stop off at Brian Smith's to buy jugs of the best cider around. Every farm stand has something amazing: huge Cinderella pumpkins, handsome thick-skinned squashes, hardy greens, mighty root vegetables pulled from the earth—gnarly carrots, dirty beets and potatoes, rutabagas and white turnips—and cabbages and brussels sprouts, all made sweeter by the first frosts of the season. The onions are splendid—bulbous ones, long ones, flat ones, small ones, all in colorful papery jackets. Baskets of meaty fall mushrooms sit next to pale orange persimmons on their way toward a deeper shade of ripe.

Even the grocery stores, dreary most of the year, have come to life with the glorious foods we all love to cook—big fresh hams, capons, ducks, turkeys and geese; standing rib roasts and magnificent crown roasts of pork; shellfish and salt cod. The baking aisles swell with cans of pumpkin pie filling, sacks of

flours, tins of baking soda, bottles of extracts and spices, packages of choc-
olates, tubs of candied fruits, and jars of colorful cookie decorations. All signs
indicate it's time to start cooking. And we do.

Christopher arrives one morning with a plump chicken—a bird with a
pedigree: grass-fed and the farmer's darling. So we start a big pot of her Triple X Chicken Broth to simmer on the back burners of our apartment-size
stoves. By noon, we've got enough rich broth for a simple lunch of chicken
noodle soup, with plenty left over to freeze for another day. We plan long-
range and make our golden fruitcakes in late November so we'll have time to
give them a daily drizzle of booze before we give them as gifts in December.
Melissa will follow her family tradition and spend a day making a *bûche de
Noël* with her daughters.

Friends stop in wanting to visit, catch up, share a story, ask our advice
about something they want to cook. Sometimes they come bearing gifts, like
our friend Neal, who loads us up with his neat bundles of oak for our stove.
Or Teresa, who showed up one day carrying a potted lemon tree in one hand
and a bag of homemade cookies in the other. Andrew will drop in with a brace
of pheasant or news of venison to come. And Steve might stop by to get our
take on some new flavors that he's developing for his line of salumi. We offer
a tea or glass of something stronger. There's usually something going on the
stove or resting on the counter and we offer that too. The visit wouldn't feel
right if we didn't have something delicious to serve them and a small gift to
send off with them.

Foods of the holidays are classics, tied to tradition and memory. We cook
our grandmothers', aunts', and mothers' recipes to bring them to life and in-
vite the people we miss to the table again. For us, it wouldn't be a holiday
without Neenie's Sourdough-Sage Stuffing, or Jim's Roast Capon, or Peggy's
Grand Marnier Soufflé. But no matter what your menu, the most important
thing is to join together for a meal and share the intimacy of the table. The
recipes in this book are our gift to you.

Christopher *&* Melissa

it's always five o'clock somewhere

GETTING DRUNK

by

Colman Andrews

I like to drink. This is no secret to anyone who knows me. Let's define
some terms, here, though: I don't live in a constant state of intoxication.
I don't—I can't—work drunk. I don't get drunk every night, or even necessar-
ily every week. I don't get drunk on purpose. I mean, I know that alcohol will
inebriate me if I consume a certain quantity of it, and in fact appreciate that
quality in it, but I don't sit down at the table, open a bottle of whisky, and say
"Boy, am I gonna get blotto tonight!"

And when I talk about getting drunk, incidentally, I don't mean falling-
down/throwing-up/screaming-and-flailing-or-sniffling-and-sobbing/out-of-
control drunk. I mean drinking to the point that the chemical equilibrium of
my body begins to be altered in various noticeable ways—my capillaries di-
lated, my muscles relaxed, my neurons disordered—all with pleasurable effect.

Drinking is not an obsession with me. It is far from the defining activity
of my life. I don't wake up in the morning imagining what alcoholic beverages
I will consume that day. Unlike an old friend of mine—an English writer born
in Texas, now living in France, no less—I don't feel sad when I realize that I've
had my last drink of the day. Drinking is simply a thing I do, a part of the mix. I
drink wine with dinner most nights, rarely (these days) more than half a bottle
or so, sometimes but by no means always preceded by a cocktail. The other
nights, I might have a small whisky when I come home or a brandy before I go
to bed, or I might have nothing at all. I almost never drink at lunchtime, unless
I'm off somewhere where lunchtime drinking is the norm. Occasionally, day or
night, circumstances permitting, I exceed these limits.

I don't drive drunk, but I'd be a liar if I said that I have never driven drunk.
I was lucky (as were those on the road around me); I was blessed. And I don't

intend to count on luck or blessings anymore. Sometimes, I came to realize some years ago, when we drink more than we've intended to, judgment and coordination take advantage of the situation and sneak off hand-in-hand in the middle of the party, so discreetly that we don't even notice that they're gone. One of the drinker's most important responsibilities is to keep an eye on them, even through the haze—and to shut the bash down (and give up the car keys) if they disappear.

Though I'm well aware of both the physical dangers of alcohol and its beneficial effects (in the latter case, I'm thinking mostly of wine's apparent values to the cardiovascular system and as an anti-carcinogen), I neither drink nor moderate my drinking for medical reasons. I do moderate it—I drink less now than I did 20 or even ten years ago, and will probably drink less in 2010 than I do in 2009—but only out of common sense. My body is less resilient now than it used to be, and, since I drink for pleasure, I try to avoid drinking to the point of displeasure.

Why do I drink, then? Because I like the way alcohol smells and tastes, especially in the forms in which I most often encounter it, which are (in approximately this order) wine, tequila, whisky, martinis and negronis, various brandies, and a very occasional beer, usually a very cold one in very hot weather. Because I like the trappings of imbibing, the company it keeps—the restaurants and cafés and bars and (usually) the people who gather in them. And—back to getting drunk—because I frankly like the way alcohol makes me feel. I like the glow, the softening of hard edges, the faint anesthesia. I like the way my mind races, one zigzag step ahead of logic. I like the flash flood of unexpected utter joy that sometimes courses quickly through me. I like the feeling of being almost but not quite in control.

NEGRONI
makes 2

A negroni is a simple combination of equal parts Campari, sweet vermouth, and gin. We've ordered negronis in unlikely places, once in a plasticky Eurasian disco bar in Taipei. How hard could it be for a bartender to screw it up? The formula is so simple and relies completely on the guaranteed goodness of what's in the bottles themselves. But you'd be surprised. We've had them arrive in water goblets packed with so much ice you'd think we'd ordered iced tea, or shaken so vigorously they looked like tropical pink smoothies. We're happiest when it is made elegant, aperitif size, in a stemless glass with just a couple of large rocks and a sliver of orange, more rind than flesh. Its digestive qualities makes it a perfect drink to stimulate the appetite.

1½ ounces gin	1½ ounces Campari
1½ ounces sweet vermouth	2 small orange slivers

Pour the gin, sweet vermouth, and Campari into a tall glass and stir gently. Pour into two short glasses with a couple of large ice cubes in each. Rub the rims of the glasses with the slivers of orange, then add an orange sliver to each.

✦ For a Straight Negroni, if you love the bitter flavor of Campari but don't want the alcohol, fill a glass with ice and add a bottle of San Pellegrino's Sanbitter, a splash of club soda, and a slice of orange.

JACK MANHATTAN
makes 2

We make these when we're in the mood to sip something dark and husky. Others may prefer smooth bourbon, but we like the slightly rougher edge of Jack Daniel's against the sweet vermouth and the booze soaked cherry at the end.

4 ounces Jack Daniel's whiskey	2 dashes Angostura bitters
1½ ounces sweet vermouth	2 maraschino cherries

Put a big handful of ice cubes into a large glass. Add the whiskey, sweet vermouth, and bitters and stir gently. Strain into two chilled stemmed cocktail glasses, if you like that look, or into two lowball glasses; add a cherry to each.

WORKING UP AN APPETITE

FRIED ZUCCHINI
serves 6

Dusting the zucchini with flour before dipping it into the batter helps the batter cling, which makes for a delicious puffy coating. Zucchini deep-fried this way are irresistible; even the vegetable-finicky (kids or adults) won't turn their noses up at these.

1½ cups all-purpose flour
Salt
1–2 cups white wine
4–6 medium zucchini

Canola, peanut, or corn oil
1 lemon, halved
Small handful parsley leaves, chopped

For the batter, whisk 1 cup of the flour and ½ teaspoon salt together in a medium bowl. Gradually add 1 cup of the wine, whisking until the batter is smooth. The batter should be about the consistency of heavy cream; thin it with a little more wine if it is too thick. Set the batter aside.

Put the remaining ½ cup flour into another medium bowl and season it with a good pinch or two of salt. Cut the zucchini in half crosswise, then lengthwise into fat sticks.

Add enough oil to a heavy pot or wok to reach a depth of 2 inches. Heat the oil over medium heat until it registers 350° on a candy thermometer.

Working in small batches, dredge the zucchini in the seasoned flour, then toss the pieces into a sieve and shake off the excess flour. Give the reserved batter a quick stir. Dip the lightly floured zucchini into the batter, shaking off any excess. Carefully add the zucchini to the hot oil one piece at a time to prevent them from clumping together. Fry the zucchini in small batches, turning them as they brown, until puffed and golden all over, about 5 minutes. Use a slotted spatula to lift the zucchini out of the oil, then drain the pieces on paper towels. Season with salt while still hot.

Serve the zucchini in the small batches as you fry so it stays hot and crisp. They are quite delicious with a squeeze of lemon juice and garnished with chopped parsley.

BEANS WITH SAUSAGES AND TUNA
serves 6

We like to use baby lima, great Northern, navy, or cannellini beans for this dish. Simmer the beans slowly, gently rehydrating them. That way they are less likely to overcook and have their skins split open.

2 cups dried white beans, soaked for a few hours or overnight

1 onion, halved

1 clove garlic

3 bay leaves

Salt

One 8–12-ounce piece fresh tuna

Really good extra-virgin olive oil

A few black peppercorns

1 lemon

6–8 sausages

Pepper

1 handful parsley leaves, chopped

Drain the beans and put them into a medium, heavy-bottomed pot. Cover them with cold water by 2 inches or so. Add the onions, garlic, and 2 of the bay leaves. Bring the beans just to a simmer over medium heat, stirring occasionally. Reduce the heat to low and very gently simmer them until they are swollen and tender, 30–90 minutes depending on the freshness of the dried beans. Remove the pot from the heat. Stir a generous pinch of salt into the beans. Let them cool to just warm or to room temperature in the cooking liquid. (The beans will keep in the refrigerator for up to 4 days.)

Season the tuna with salt, put it into a small pot, and barely cover it with olive oil. Add the remaining bay leaf, the peppercorns, and a strip or two of zest from the lemon. Poach the tuna over low heat until it turns pale and is just cooked through, 10–15 minutes. Remove the pot from the heat and let the tuna cool to just warm or to room temperature in the poaching oil. (The tuna will keep in the refrigerator for up to 4 days. Discard the aromatics before storing it and let the tuna and oil come to room temperature before serving.)

Grill the sausages over a hot charcoal fire or gas grill until they are browned and crusty all over and cooked through, about 10 minutes.

Drain the beans, discarding the onions and garlic, and transfer them to a serving platter. Season them with salt and pepper. Arrange the sausages and the tuna over the beans. Moisten the beans with some of the poaching oil from the tuna. Scatter the chopped parsley on top and serve with wedges of lemon.

MUSHROOMS ON TOAST
serves 2–4

Our friend Patty Curtan, a wonderful cook and artist, was working with us for a few days at Canal House when chanterelle season arrived in our neck of the woods. Early one morning I found two handfuls of mushrooms, enough to get excited about, but hardly enough to make a meal for the three of us. By late morning we were starving, so I quickly sautéed the mushrooms and served them over thick slices of buttered toast. That got our appetites going for more. But it wasn't until early fall, long after Patty had gone back to the West Coast, that I landed on the mother lode. Up over a ridge on a dark wooded slope I came upon a virtual field of "blooming" golden mushrooms. It took less than 15 minutes to gather all that I could fit in my bag—nearly 20 pounds! With those we made a wild mushroom ragù, like the one on the next page, and ate like kings for a week. —— MH

Melt 3 tablespoons butter and 1 tablespoon olive oil together in a skillet over medium heat. Add a minced clove of garlic and ¾ pound cleaned halved mushrooms. Season with salt and pepper. Sauté the mushrooms, stirring occasionally, until they have released their juices, about 5 minutes. Stir in ¼ cup heavy cream and a handful of chopped parsley leaves and cook for a tiny bit longer. Serve mushrooms and their creamy juices spooned over hot buttered toast.

MUSHROOM RAGÙ ON POLENTA
serves 6–8

We love all sorts of mushroom varieties and this stew lends itself to using a mixture of different shapes, textures, and flavors. If you don't have time to make polenta, serve the ragù over thick slices of crusty toast that have been lightly rubbed with a peeled clove of garlic. Set a poached egg on top of each and grate some parmigiano-reggiano or pecorino over the eggs.

FOR THE POLENTA
I cup polenta
Salt
2 tablespoons butter

FOR THE RAGÙ
2 tablespoons extra-virgin olive oil
4 tablespoons butter
I small onion, chopped
I clove garlic, minced

2 pounds mixed wild and/or cultivated mushrooms, cleaned and halved or quartered
Leaves of 4 thyme sprigs
2 tablespoons sherry
4 canned whole peeled plum tomatoes
2 cups chicken stock
½ bunch parsley, leaves chopped
Salt and pepper

For the polenta, put 5 cups of cold water into a medium, heavy-bottomed pot. Stir in the polenta and 2 generous pinches of salt. Bring to a boil over medium-high heat, stirring often. Reduce the heat to medium-low and cook the polenta, stirring occasionally, until it is tender, 45–60 minutes. Don't underestimate the time it takes to cook polenta—about an hour for the corn-meal to fully soften. The polenta will swell and thicken as it cooks. Stir in a little more water as needed if it gets too thick before it's finished cooking. Stir in the butter and season with salt. The polenta can rest like this while the ragù is being prepared.

For the ragù, heat the olive oil and 2 tablespoons of the butter together in a large skillet over medium heat until the butter foams. Add the onions and garlic and cook until soft and translucent, 3–5 minutes. Add the mushrooms and cook, stirring occasionally, until they begin to soften, about 3 minutes. Add the thyme and sherry. Add the tomatoes, crushing them with your hand as you drop them into the mushrooms. Add the stock, parsley, and remaining 2 tablespoons of butter. Simmer the ragù over medium-low heat until it is stewy and has thickened a bit, about 20 minutes. Season with salt and pepper (it will most likely need it). Spoon the mushroom ragù over the warm polenta.

EAT YOUR VEGETABLES

BRAISED ENDIVE
serves 6

Belgian endive is pleasantly bitter and delicately crisp raw, but we like how it sweetens and becomes supple when braised this way.

4 tablespoons butter
6 Belgian endives

Salt and pepper
1 cup chicken stock

Melt 3 tablespoons of the butter in a large skillet over medium heat. Add the endives to the skillet, season with salt and pepper, and cook for a few minutes, turning them as they brown. Reduce heat to low and add stock. Cover and braise, turning endives now and then, until tender, 30–40 minutes. Uncover the skillet, increase heat to medium-high, and cook for a minute to reduce any pan juices. Swirl in the remaining tablespoon of butter. Taste for seasoning.

FENNEL GRATIN
serves 2–4

Peel off the large tough outer layer of the bulbs to get to their tender, sweeter hearts.

2 bulbs fennel, trimmed and halved
  lengthwise
2 cups whole milk
1 clove garlic
1 bay leaf

Salt and pepper
3 tablespoons butter, softened
Parmigiano-reggiano
Ground nutmeg

Arrange fennel in a medium pot in a single layer. Add milk, garlic, and bay leaf. Season with salt and pepper. Partially cover pot and gently poach the fennel over medium-low heat, turning it occasionally, until tender, about 45 minutes.

Preheat the broiler. Use 1 tablespoon of the butter to butter a gratin dish large enough to fit the fennel in a single layer. Arrange fennel in the dish cut side up. (Save milk for another use or discard it.) Grate parmigiano-reggiano over the fennel, sprinkle with a little nutmeg and pepper, and dot with remaining 2 tablespoons butter. Broil until the cheese is golden brown, 1–2 minutes.

BEETS WITH BUTTER AND TARRAGON
serves 4

We prefer roasting beets to boiling them because they retain more of their earthy "dirty" flavor cooked this way. This simple preparation barely merits a recipe, but for quantity's sake, figure about 3–4 small beets per person. Prepare more or less depending on the size of the beets and your guests' beet-loving tastes.

12 smallish beets, leaves trimmed	1 handful fresh tarragon leaves, chopped
4 tablespoons butter, melted	Salt and pepper

Preheat the oven to 400°. Wrap each beet in aluminum foil and roast in the oven until tender, 45–60 minutes. (Take the beets out of the oven, unwrap one, and pierce it with a paring knife to check if it is soft.)

Slip the skins off the beets. Halve the beets, if you like, and put them into a bowl. Toss them with the melted butter and the tarragon and season with salt and pepper.

MASHED RUTABAGAS WITH LOADS OF SCALLIONS
serves 4–6

Rutabagas, also known as swedes (swedish turnips) or yellow turnips, are kind of an old-fashioned vegetable. If you are under twenty-five it's most likely that you have never even eaten one. But we like their cabbagey-turnip flavor, though they do benefit from a little doctoring up! Sometimes we add a starchy potato or two as rutabagas can be quite watery.

Put 3 large peeled rutabagas cut into medium size pieces into a large pot of salted cold water. Add 1 peeled potato and bring to a boil over medium-high heat. Cover, reduce heat to medium-low, and cook until the rutabagas are tender, at least 60 minutes. Drain the vegetables into a colander, then return the empty pot to the heat and add 4 tablespoons of butter and a generous cup of finely chopped scallions. Sauté the scallions for about 2 minutes. Return the rutabagas and potatoes to the pot and mash with a potato masher until smooth. If they are too dry, add a splash of hot milk or cream. Season with lots of salt and pepper and add as much butter as your conscience will allow.

ROASTED RED PEPPERS WITH CURRANTS AND CAPERS
serves 4–8

It's an odd sight the first time you see someone blistering the skin of peppers (or eggplant for that matter) over the flame on a kitchen stove. We do this when our grill or little wood-burning stove isn't fired up. Charring the skins this way gives a smoky depth of flavor you don't get by roasting the peppers in the oven. But if an oven's all you've got, use it! The other flavors going on in this dish will prevail.

½ cup really good olive oil
2 tablespoons currants
1–2 tablespoons capers
Juice of 1 lemon

4 red bell peppers
1 small handful fresh mint leaves,
    torn or chopped
Salt and pepper

Put the olive oil, currants, capers, and lemon juice into a serving dish and set aside while preparing the peppers.

Set the peppers on top of the burner plates on top of a gas stove. Turn on the flame to medium-high heat. Or, set the peppers on a grill over hot coals. Char the skins of the peppers, turning them as they blister and blacken all over. (You can char the peppers in a very hot oven, 500° is a good temperature. Put the peppers on a sheet pan and roast until charred all over.) When the peppers are ready, put them into a bowl and cover them to steam and soften the fragile charred skins so they are easier to peel off. When the peppers are cool enough to handle, peel and rub off the blackened skin. Pull off the stems, tear the peppers in half, remove the cores, and scrape the seeds away from the flesh (resist the urge to rinse the seeds off. You will rinse away delicious flavor.).

Put the skinned and cleaned peppers into the dish with the olive oil. Add the mint, season with salt and pepper, and turn the peppers until they are well coated. Let them marinate for an hour or so before serving.

down & dirty

POMMES ANNA
serves 2–4

Top this galette with a pile of salad, fried eggs with harissa, or roast chicken. But they are perfect with nothing more than salt and a sprig of parsley.

4 tablespoons butter

3 all-purpose white potatoes, peeled

Salt and pepper

Sprigs of parsley, for garnish

Preheat oven to 375°. Melt 2 tablespoons of the butter in a large ovenproof nonstick skillet over medium heat. Remove the skillet from the heat.

Using a mandoline or a sharp knife, thinly slice potatoes, keeping them in the order they were sliced (this will make fanning the slices out in the skillet go more easily). Beginning in the center of the skillet, fan potato slices out, tightly overlapping them in a concentric circle, lining the bottom of the skillet. Season potatoes with salt and pepper and dot with remaining 2 tablespoons butter.

Return skillet to medium-high heat and cook potatoes until they are golden brown on the bottom, 10–15 minutes. Cover skillet with a cookie sheet. Carefully invert the potatoes onto the cookie sheet. Slide potatoes back into skillet browned side up. Transfer skillet to oven and cook until browned on the bottom, about 15 minutes. Remove from the oven and slide potatoes onto a serving platter. Season with salt and garnish with sprigs of parsley.

POTATOES ANNA
serves 4–6

We don't know why these potatoes are named after Anna. She must have been quite a gal! We suspect they are an American cousin of the French classic above.

Preheat oven to 375°. Peel 6 round all-purpose white potatoes. On a cutting board, hold the handle of a wooden spoon alongside a potato. With a sharp knife, slice through the potato, using the spoon handle as a "stop" to keep from slicing all the way through (potatoes remain whole; see picture, right). Slice all the potatoes this way. Put potatoes in a baking dish. Pour ¼ cup melted butter over them. Season with salt and pepper. Pour 2 cups chicken stock into the dish and over potatoes. Roast in the oven, basting often, until the potatoes are tender and golden on top, about 1 hour. Serve garnished with parsley leaves.

Sister Frances' Potatoes

RÖSTI (OR A VERSION THEREOF)
serves 4–6

What do you get when you cross rösti with a potato pancake and latkes? We don't know but, whatever you want to call it, it sure is good!

3 large russet potatoes, peeled	Salt
1 egg	6 tablespoons butter

Grate potatoes on the large holes of a box grater into a bowl. Add egg and 2 generous pinches of salt. Mix well.

Melt 4 tablespoons of the butter in a large nonstick skillet over medium-high heat. Add potatoes, gently pressing them with a spatula into a flat cake. Cook until the edges brown and a deep golden crust forms on the bottom, 10–15 minutes. Reduce heat if it begins to burn. Remove skillet from heat.

Cover skillet with a cookie sheet. Carefully invert the potato cake onto the cookie sheet. Return skillet to medium-high heat. Melt remaining 2 tablespoons butter in skillet. Slide potato cake back into skillet browned side up. Cook until bottom is golden, 10–15 minutes. Slide potato cake onto a large round platter. Season with salt. Slice into wedges and serve.

SISTER FRANCES' POTATOES
serves 4–6

Sister Frances, one of the last Shakers, made these potatoes for us when we visited her community at Sabbathday Lake, Maine. The preparation is simple and the finished dish elegant and delicious. The Shaker sisters weren't worried about their waistlines but if you are, use milk instead of half-and-half.

Put 4 peeled russet potatoes cut into half-inch cubes into a deep heavy medium pot. Add 4 tablespoons butter and about 2 cups half-and-half, enough to cover the potatoes. Season with salt and pepper. Bring just to a simmer over medium heat, then reduce heat to low and let cook until the potatoes are tender and have absorbed most of the half-and-half, about 60 minutes. (Keep potatoes submerged as they cook so they don't turn dark.) Stir occasionally and carefully with a rubber spatula to keep the potato pieces intact. Season with salt and pepper and garnish with a sprinkling of chopped chives.

long & slow

SERIOUS RAGÙ
makes 2–3 quarts

In the spirit of old-style Northern Italian country cooking, this ragù uses inexpensive cuts of pork, lamb, and beef. These tough cuts are full of flavor but need a long slow cooking to tenderize the meat. The time it takes is worth it as this sauce is seriously delicious. We believe in making a big batch and freezing it in dinner-size portions (allow about 1 cup per person to serve over pasta).

2 pounds lamb necks or shoulder lamb chops
2 pounds pork spareribs
2 pounds beef short ribs
Salt and pepper
Olive oil
1 large yellow onion, diced
1 large carrot, peeled and finely diced
2 ribs celery, finely diced

2 cloves garlic, sliced
5 anchovy fillets, chopped
A healthy grating of nutmeg
1–2 cups white wine
One 28-ounce can crushed tomatoes
One 15-ounce can plain tomato sauce
Handful of fresh parsley leaves, finely chopped

Use paper towel to dry the meat. Season with salt and pepper. Heat a little oil in very large heavy pot. Brown meat in batches over medium-high heat, removing it from the pot as it browns. Continue until all the meat is browned.

Add a little more oil to the pot. Add the onions, carrots, celery, garlic, and anchovies. Cook, stirring often, for about 5 minutes. Season with salt and pepper, and nutmeg. Add the wine and cook for about 3 minutes.

Return the browned meat to the pot. Add the crushed tomatoes and tomato sauce along with 2 cups of water. Bring to a simmer, then reduce heat to low and slowly simmer the ragù for about 3 hours. Give it a stir from time to time and add more water if it looks like it is getting too thick.

Remove all the large pieces of meat from the pot to a large cutting board. Discard all the bones and gristle and any of the meat that you don't like the look of. Finely chop the remaining meat and return it to the pot.

Put the pot on the stove over low heat and barely simmer the ragù for another 2 hours. Continue to add water if the sauce gets too thick. Just before serving, add parsley. Serve over pasta with grated parmigiano-reggiano, if you like.

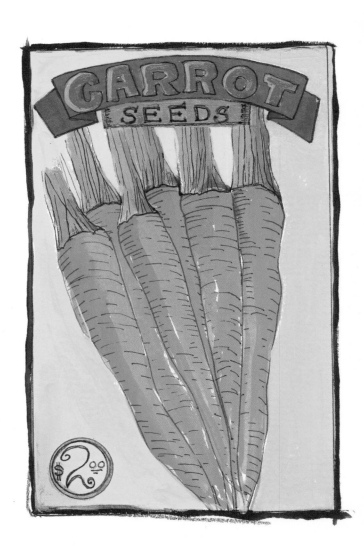

BEEF WITH CARROTS
serves 4

This is our take on *boeuf bourguignon* cum *boeuf aux carottes*. We made some changes. We are not fans of marinating meat in wine. It kind of pickles (or cooks) the meat, leaving it strangely dry. So we don't. And we cut the meat into big pieces and serve one or two per person.

This recipe is simply a great stew. Even though it seems fussy to remove all the meat and carrots at the end, skim off the fat, then strain and reduce the sauce, it really makes a difference—your sauce will be smooth and silky.

One 2-pound chuck steak, cut into 8–12 pieces
Salt and pepper
½ cup flour
2 tablespoons olive oil
2 medium yellow onions, sliced
1 clove garlic, sliced

4 anchovy fillets, minced
6 prunes, pitted and chopped
Handful of chopped fresh parsley leaves
2 pounds carrots, peeled and cut into 1-inch pieces
2 cups chicken stock
1 cup red wine

Preheat the oven to 300°. Season the meat with salt and pepper. Roll the beef in the flour and shake off any excess. Heat the oil over medium heat in a heavy pot with a lid. Add the beef and brown it on all sides then remove it from the pot. Add the onions, garlic, and anchovies to the pot and cook until the onions are soft and translucent, about 10 minutes.

Return the beef to the pot and add the prunes, parsley, carrots, chicken stock, and wine. Bring it to a simmer over medium-high heat, cover, put it in the oven, and cook until the meat is tender, 2–3 hours. Remove from the oven.

Use a slotted spoon to transfer all the meat and vegetables to a bowl. Using a big spoon, skim the fat off the surface of the sauce. Strain the sauce through a fine sieve into a bowl, pushing any solids through the screen. Return the strained sauce to the pot and cook over medium-high heat until it thickens slightly. Return the meat and carrots to the pot. Taste for seasoning. Serve with hot buttered noodles.

LAMB SHOULDER COOKED IN RED WINE
serves 4–6

I am not sure where my mother came up with adding coffee to the pan juices when roasting lamb. She *said* it was a trick that she learned from a Swedish friend, but truth was, Mom was an improviser. More likely there was an extra cup of coffee on the counter when the roast needed a splash of liquid and with her what-the-hell attitude (she was the mother of five), she may have just tossed it in. No matter, it adds good rich flavor to the sauce. —— CH

One 3–4-pound boned, rolled, and tied lamb shoulder roast
Salt and pepper
Olive oil
1 yellow onion, chopped
1 carrot, peeled and chopped
1 rib celery, chopped

2 branches fresh rosemary
6 prunes, pitted and chopped
6 juniper berries
2 cups red wine
1 small cup espresso or very strong black coffee

Preheat the oven to 325°. Season the lamb generously with salt and pepper. Heat a few tablespoons of oil in a heavy large pot with a lid over medium-high heat. Add the lamb and brown well on all sides, about 10 minutes. Remove the lamb from the pot and set aside.

Add a little more oil to the pot, if necessary, then add the onions, carrots, and celery. Cook the vegetables, stirring from time to time, until soft, about 10 minutes. Season with salt and pepper. Add the rosemary, prunes, juniper berries, wine, and coffee.

Return the lamb to the pot, cover and cook in the oven until the lamb is very tender, about 2 hours.

Lift the lamb from the pot and set on a cutting board. Cover with a piece of foil while it rests. Skim off any fat on the surface of the sauce. Remove and discard the rosemary and juniper berries. Strain the sauce into a bowl, pressing the solids through a fine mesh sieve. Return the sauce to the pot and cook over medium-high heat until it thickens slightly and has reduced to about 2 cups. Season with salt and pepper.

Remove the string from the lamb and thinly slice. Arrange on a platter and spoon the sauce over the lamb. Garnish with rosemary, if you like.

BREAST OF VEAL BRAISED WITH CHILES
serves 4

Breast of veal is one of the cheapest cuts of meat around. Of course, there is a whole lot of bone and cartilage attached to that meat (see the picture on the opposite page). But that is what makes it taste so good.

8 poblano chiles

One 5–6-pound breast of veal

2 tablespoons ground cumin

Salt and pepper

Olive oil

3 large yellow onions, sliced

3 cloves garlic, sliced

One 15-ounce can whole peeled plum tomatoes

Large handful of chopped fresh epazote or chopped fresh cilantro leaves

Set the chiles on top of the burner plates on top of a gas stove. Turn on the flame to medium-high heat. Or, set the chiles on a grill over hot coals. Char the skins of the chiles, turning them as they blister and blacken all over. (You can also do this in a very hot oven, 500° is a good temperature. Put the chiles on a sheet pan and roast until charred all over.) When the chiles are charred all over, put them into a bowl and cover them to let the fragile charred skins steam and soften so they are easier to peel off. When the chiles are cool enough to handle, peel and rub off the blackened skin. Pull off the stems, tear the chiles in half, remove the cores, and scrape the seeds away from the flesh (resist the urge to rinse the seeds off. You will rinse away delicious flavor.) Slice the chiles into thick strips.

Preheat the oven to 325°. Rub the veal breast all over with cumin and a generous amount of salt and pepper. Heat a few tablespoons of oil in a large heavy pot with a cover over medium-high heat. (If the roast is too big, use a heavy roasting pan and you can cover it with foil.) Add the veal and brown it well on both sides, about 10 minutes. Remove it from the pot and set aside.

Add a little more oil to the pot then add the onions and garlic. Reduce heat to medium, and cook, stirring from time to time, until the vegetables are soft and translucent, about 20 minutes. Add the chiles and tomatoes to the pot, crushing the tomatoes with your hand. Put the veal bone side down into the pot.

continued

Cover and cook in the oven until the veal is very tender, about 4 hours. Remove the lid for the last hour of cooking.

Remove the pot from the oven and turn off the heat. Transfer the veal to a cutting board. Remove and discard the rib bones, connective tissue, gristle, and any large pieces of fat.

Transfer the chiles and onions from the pot to a bowl with a slotted spoon. Skim off any fat on the surface of the pan juices. Strain the pan juices through a fine mesh sieve then return the sauce to the pot. Cook over medium-high heat until the sauce has reduced and thickened, about 10 minutes. Return the chiles and onions to the pot. Place the veal on top. Cover and return it to the still warm oven to keep it hot.

Just before serving, slice the meat on a cutting board, then arrange it on a platter with the onions and chiles. Spoon the sauce on top. Garnish with epazote or lots of chopped cilantro. Serve with a stack of warm corn tortillas, and a big green salad with lots of sliced avocados, if you like.

"When I see a bird that walks like a duck, and swims like a duck, and quacks like a duck, I call that bird a duck."—*James Whitcomb Riley*

QUACK

QUACK

QUACK

QUACK

QUACK

QUACK

ROAST DUCK AND POTATOES
serves 4–6

This duck dish flies in the face of elaborate restaurant theater—Roasted Duck Served Two Ways in which the duck is presented to the table. Then the rosy pink breasts are carved from the carcass tableside, after which the duck is whisked back to the kitchen where the legs and thighs are returned to the oven to roast until perfectly tender. Finally, the waiter returns to the table for the final act. That's a lot of dinner theater.

Our recipe is just as delicious and more doable for us home cooks. And it's really a two-in-one dish. Roasted crispy-skinned duck with fully cooked tender meat plus potatoes roasted in duck fat. Each one satisfying enough to make a meal in itself, together they are heaven.

One 5–6 pound duck	Salt
1 tablespoon olive oil	12 medium all-purpose white
1 tablespoon anise seeds	potatoes, peeled

Preheat the oven to 400°. Rinse the duck, pat it dry, and trim off the wingtips and any excess neck skin. Prick the skin all over. Rub the olive oil and anise seeds all over the duck, then season the bird inside and out with salt. Tie the legs together with kitchen string.

Put the duck into a large roasting pan breast side up. Add ½ cup water to the pan. Roast the duck in the oven for 30 minutes. Remove the pan from the oven. The duck may stick to the bottom of the pan so use a metal spatula to get under the duck to release it. Settle the duck back into the pan and add the potatoes, nestling them around the duck.

Reduce the oven temperature to 375°. Return the roasting pan with the duck and potatoes to the oven. Turn the potatoes from time to time so they develop a deep golden crusty skin as they roast. (The potatoes may also stick to the roasting pan, so carefully release them from the bottom of the pan as you turn them, keeping the crust attached to the potato.)

Roast the duck and potatoes for another 30–50 minutes, until the duck skin is crisp all over and the potatoes are deep golden brown and tender when pierced. Transfer duck and potatoes to a serving platter and season with salt.

Dear M,

So today was the day to drag all the flotsam and jetsam out of the upstairs rooms to make the way ready for the painters who arrive on Monday. I guess I did the wrong thing and began to drill down, editing family pictures from a big messy box of my mother's, weeding out the linen closet, and finally reorganizing my Rolodex. The whole house was/is topsy-turvy and Jim was out of his mind and hammering home his point—over and over! But mid all this I came downstairs to try to put something on the stove so we could eat. I dragged out a duck and calmly cut it up and began to cook it. But then came a stroke of genius. I opened a tin of sardines and sautéed the duck liver with a few scallions. I pulled out a delicious fresh box of club crackers and made Jim a little love token of crax with sardines and crax with duck liver. Now he's in the palm of my hand. You may need this trick someday. xoxoxo, C

—— *an e-mail sent from CH to MH*

DUCK WITH TURNIPS AND RICE
serves 6

We first ate this in Valencia, Spain's paella country. We had lunch under a tree in the garden of a rice farmer surrounded by his fields. His wife made his favorite dish, a classic duck with turnips, white beans, and rice. We remember that day every time we make this simpler version of her meal.

One 5–6 pound duck, cut into
   10 pieces
Salt and pepper
Olive oil
2 slices pancetta, finely chopped
3 cloves garlic, sliced

4 white turnips, peeled and quartered
5 cups chicken stock
1 teaspoon pimentón
Pinch of saffron threads, crumbled
½ preserved lemon, rind only, minced
1½ cups short-grain rice

Season the duck on all sides with salt and pepper. Heat some olive oil in a paella pan or in a large skillet over medium-high heat. Put the duck skin side down in the pan and cook until very brown, about 15 minutes. Turn the duck over, add the pancetta, garlic, and turnips. Continue to cook, turning the turnips as they brown, about 20 minutes. Reduce heat to low.

Meanwhile, heat stock in a pot, along with the pimentón, saffron, and preserved lemon, over medium heat until just simmering. Cover and turn off the heat.

Add the rice to the pan. Make sure it is evenly distributed. Add the hot stock and cook until the rice is tender and has absorbed the stock, about 25 minutes. Let rest about 20 minutes. Serve with fresh lemon wedges, if you like.

DUCK WITH APPLES AND ONIONS
serves 6

Once when I was photographing a book with Jacques Pépin, he prepared braised duck. As I looked through the lens of the camera and clicked away I saw more than the pictures I was taking. I saw how to cook a duck so that the skin is perfectly crisp. Thank you, Jacques. We dedicate this recipe to you. —— CH

One 5–6 pound duck, cut into
    8–10 pieces, including skin and
    fat, diced
Salt and pepper
4 small onions, halved lengthwise

4 apples, peeled, cored, and quartered
Handful of chopped fresh sage
    leaves, plus a few whole leaves
    for garnish
½ cup port

Season the duck on all sides with salt and pepper. Arrange the duck skin side down in a large skillet with a cover. Scatter the skin and fat around the duck. Cook over medium-high heat (resist the temptation to turn the duck; leave it skin side down the whole time) until the duck is very well browned, about 20 minutes. Leave the duck skin side down, reduce heat to low, cover, and cook for 45 minutes more. Transfer the duck and all the cracklings from the skillet to a platter with a slotted spatula. Allow the duck to rest.

Add the onions cut side down along with the apples and the sage to the skillet with all the duck fat and juices. Increase the heat to medium-high and brown the onions and apples, taking care to keep the onion halves whole, about 10 minutes. Reduce the heat to medium-low, cover, and cook until the apples and onions are tender, about 15 minutes more. Remove the onions and apples from the skillet and arrange them around the duck.

Pour off and discard the fat from the skillet. Add the port to the skillet and cook, using a wooden spoon to scrape up any browned bits from the bottom of the skillet. Pour the sauce over the duck. Garnish with fresh sage leaves.

VARIATION: For a richer sauce, add 1 cup of heavy cream to the skillet after adding the port. Increase the heat to medium-high and cook, stirring with a wooden spoon, for 5 minutes. Strain the sauce over the duck. Garnish with fresh sage leaves.

POACHED DUCK EGGS ON BITTER GREENS
serves 2–4

Duck eggs are larger with richer yolks than the average chicken egg. Their flavor is more pronounced, more "eggy". We buy them whenever we see them at local farm markets. Bitter greens like chicory, frisée, and radicchio, to name a few, are sturdy enough to stand up to the richness of the eggs and the warm dressing.

4 thick slices bacon

1 clove garlic, thinly sliced

2 cups large cubes of bread

Salt and pepper

4 duck eggs

3 tablespoons red wine vinegar

A small spoonful Dijon mustard

3–4 tablespoons extra-virgin olive oil

6–8 cups bitter salad greens

Fry the bacon in a medium skillet over medium heat until crisp, about 10 minutes. Drain the bacon on paper towels, leaving rendered bacon fat in the skillet. Pour a couple of tablespoons of the bacon fat into a small bowl and set aside.

Return the skillet with the bacon fat to medium heat. Add garlic, the bread cubes, and season well with salt and pepper. (If there is not enough bacon fat left in the skillet, add a little olive oil.) Toast the bread cubes, turning them often, until golden and crisp all over, about 5 minutes. Put the croutons into a large salad or mixing bowl. Set the skillet aside.

Bring a deep medium pan of salted water to a gentle simmer over medium heat. Crack an egg into a small cup or saucer, then gently slip the egg into the simmering water. Repeat with the remaining eggs. Poach the eggs until the whites turn, well, until they turn white (or opaque) while the yolks remain soft, about 5 minutes. Transfer the eggs with a slotted spoon to paper towels to drain.

Return the skillet to medium heat. Stir in the vinegar with a wooden spoon, deglazing the skillet, then stir in the mustard. Add reserved bacon fat and the olive oil. Swirl the skillet over the heat until the vinaigrette is nice and warm.

Add the greens to the bowl with the croutons, add the warm vinaigrette, and toss well. Taste the salad and adjust the seasoning. Divide the salad between two to four plates and top each salad with eggs and bacon.

pears, apples & chocolate

PEAR SORBET
makes 1 quart

Early one spring some years ago when my husband and I bought our home, we barely noticed that it came with a couple of fruit-bearing trees in the back yard. By the fall of that year we discovered one of the trees was loaded with gnarly-looking green pears. We waited until they felt ripe before picking them, then laid them out to finish ripening. But the pears bypassed tender and juicy, and decided to go straight to rot. I figured our sweet little tree was a bum variety for eating pears. The following year we gave the pears another try, this time picking the fruit when it was hard and unripe. We wrapped the pears in paper and stored them in a cool, dark spot in the garage. Lo and behold, it worked. The fruit ripened slowly. I began cooking with the pears, making cobblers and tarts, jars of thick pear sauce, and roasting them in a skillet with pork chops or sausages. But the preparation we've come to love the most is this pear sorbet. It tastes like the best pear in the world, sweet and perfumed, crisp, cold and refreshing. —— MH

1 cup sugar   ⅓ cup pear brandy
5 ripe, juicy pears

Make a simple syrup by putting the sugar and ½ cup water into a heavy-bottomed saucepan. Cook over medium-low heat, gently swirling the pan over the heat to dissolve the sugar as it melts.

When the syrup comes to a boil, cover the pan to let the steam run down the sides, washing away and dissolving any sugar granules on the sides of the pan, and cook for 2–3 minutes. Allow the syrup to cool to room temperature. You should have 1 cup of simple syrup.

Peel, quarter, and core the pears. Purée the pears in a food processor until smooth, then transfer the purée to a medium bowl. You should have about 3 cups of purée. Stir in the simple syrup and the brandy.

Freeze the pear purée in an ice cream maker following the manufacturer's instructions. Scoop the sorbet (it will have the consistency of soft-serve ice cream) into a quart container with a lid. Cover and place in the freezer for a couple of hours until it is firm. The sorbet improves with age. It will keep in the freezer for up to 1 week.

APPLE PIE
serves 6–8

When it comes to apple pie, though people may rave on about the crust, it really is all about the apples. Check out your local orchard and find the farmer's favorite; he may have an old variety that is perfect for pies. We like Honey Crisp, Cortland, Golden Delicious, Pippin, Gala, and Granny Smith because they hold their shape and keep their sweet tang as they bake.

FOR THE CRUST
1½ cups flour
Salt
8 tablespoons cold unsalted butter, cut into small pieces
2 tablespoons cold vegetable shortening

FOR THE APPLE FILLING
5–6 apples, peeled, cored, and sliced
½ cup sugar
1 teaspoon ground cinnamon
1 teaspoon vanilla extract
3 tablespoons butter, melted

For the crust, whisk the flour and a pinch of salt in a large mixing bowl. Blend in the butter and vegetable shortening with a pastry blender or a fork until crumbly. It should resemble coarse cornmeal. Sprinkle with 5 tablespoons ice water and toss lightly. Form into a ball. Don't overhandle. Wrap dough in plastic wrap and chill for at least an hour.

Preheat the oven to 375°. Roll out the dough on a lightly floured surface into a 12-inch round. Roll dough loosely around the rolling pin and place into a 9-inch deep-dish pie pan. Lightly press the dough into the pan. Trim the excess dough from the edge with a sharp knife leaving about 1 inch hanging over the edge. Tuck the dough under itself then use your thumb and forefinger to crimp the edge.

For the apple filling, mix together the apples, sugar, cinnamon, vanilla, and melted butter in a large bowl. Toss everything together until well coated. Fill the unbaked pie shell by arranging the apples in concentric circles, starting in the middle and working outward, building layers. Bake until the apples are soft and their edges are golden, about 1 hour.

CHOCOLATE GINGERBREAD
serves 12

We aren't gooey cake fans so this cake is perfect for us—more about flavor than sweetness. The gooiest part is pouring on the melted chocolate icing. We smooth it out and just let it run over the sides of the cake. Who can resist warm gingerbread on a cold fall afternoon?

FOR THE GINGERBREAD
2½ cups flour
2 teaspoons baking soda
½ teaspoon salt
1 tablespoon ground ginger
1 teaspoon ground cinnamon
1 teaspoon ground allspice
1 teaspoon dry mustard
½ teaspoon ground black pepper

8 tablespoons unsalted butter, softened
¼ cup dark brown sugar
2 eggs
1 cup molasses or sorghum
8 ounces chocolate chips, melted
1 cup espresso or strong coffee, cooled

FOR THE CHOCOLATE ICING
8 ounces chocolate chips
½ cup heavy cream

For the gingerbread, preheat the oven to 375°. Grease a 9-inch springform cake pan, then dust it with flour, tapping out any excess.

Sift or whisk the flour, baking soda, salt, ginger, cinnamon, allspice, mustard, and pepper together in a large bowl then set aside.

Put the butter into a large mixing bowl and beat with an electric mixer on medium speed until light and fluffy. Gradually beat in the brown sugar, about 2 minutes. Beat in the eggs one at a time. Beat in the molasses and the chocolate until smooth. Add the dry ingredients and the espresso alternately while you continue to beat the mixture. Use a rubber spatula to help incorporate any batter on the bottom or sides of the bowl. Pour into the prepared cake pan and bake until the top springs back when you lightly press it in the middle, about 40 minutes. Remove from the oven and place on a rack to cool.

For the chocolate icing, while the cake cools, heat the chocolate and the cream together in a small heavy pot over low heat. Stir with a whisk as it melts.

Transfer the cooled gingerbread onto to a plate. Arrange strips of waxed paper under the edges of the cake to keep the plate clean. Smooth the icing on top of the gingerbread, allowing it to drip over the sides. Remove the paper.

holiday baking

CURRANT GINGERSNAPS
makes 3–4 dozen

Every fall I get a call from my mother in the Northeast Kingdom of Vermont. "What can I send you for the holidays?" she asks. And every year the requested list is always the same—Currant Gingersnaps, her Shortbread (we call it Galette Bretonne), and Pain d'Épice. She packs up her gift boxes so well that even her delicate mint meringues arrive intact. And just as her mother—my grandmother Mimime—did for me, and my brothers and sister, Mum always tosses in net bags full of gold-wrapped chocolate coins for my girls. We treasure every morsel. —— MH

4½ cups flour
4 teaspoons baking soda
2 teaspoons salt
2 teaspoons ground ginger
1 teaspoon ground cinnamon
½ teaspoon ground cloves

¾ pound (24 tablespoons) unsalted butter, softened
1½ cups granulated sugar
1 cup dark brown sugar
2 eggs
½ cup molasses
3 cups currants

Sift or whisk the flour, baking soda, salt, ginger, cinnamon, and cloves together in a large bowl. Put the butter, 1 cup of the granulated sugar, and the brown sugar into another large mixing bowl and beat with an electric mixer on medium speed until light and fluffy. Add the eggs one at a time, then add the molasses and beat until smooth. Add the flour mixture to the butter mixture, stirring with a wooden spoon until well mixed. Stir in the currants. Wrap dough in plastic wrap and refrigerate for at least 30 minutes or up to 1 day.

Preheat the oven to 375°. Pinch off walnut-size pieces of the dough and roll into balls. Roll the balls in the remaining ½ cup sugar. Place the dough balls on a parchment paper–lined cookie sheet about 1 inch apart. Bake the cookies until cracked on top and browned on the bottom, 8–10 minutes. Cool the cookies on a rack. They will keep in an airtight container for up to 2 weeks.

SHORTBREAD
(Galette Bretonne)
makes 12

These buttery shortbread cookies are a holiday perennial at our house—my mother sends them to us in her Christmas care package. Somewhere along the line they erroneously picked up the name Galette Bretonne, which refers to the little buttery golden cookies from Brittany. This recipe makes a classic Scottish shortbread. Whatever you call them, they are delicious and now we make them all year long at Canal House. —— MH

2 cups flour
½ cup granulated sugar
1 teaspoon vanilla extract

½ pound (16 tablespoons) butter, cut into pieces
Powdered sugar

Preheat the oven to 350°. Put the flour and granulated sugar into a mixing bowl and whisk to combine. Stir in the vanilla, breaking up the bits with your fingertips. Using two butter knives, a pastry blender, or your fingers, work the butter into the flour until it is crumbly and has the texture of coarse meal.

Spread the crumbly flour-butter mixture out in an 8-inch round false-bottom tart pan, smoothing it into an even layer with your hand. Press the crumbly mixture into the pan so that the crumbs are all lightly packed together. Using a fork, gently press a shallow impression of the tines into the pastry around the edge and lightly score the surface of the galette.

Bake until pale golden brown, about 30 minutes. Remove from the oven and cut into 12 wedges in the pan while it's still warm. Let the galette cool on a rack. Dust with powdered sugar.

PAIN D'ÉPICE
makes 1 loaf

This French spice bread recipe was handed down to my mother from her mother, a native Parisian. It has a dark, almost gingerbread-like flavor and curiously not a single spice in it. Perhaps the spices were lost in translation over the years. We're not sure, but Mimime's recipe lives on with us just as it is, and we like it better than any other pain d'épice around. —— MH

1 tablespoon butter, softened

3 cups flour, plus more for dusting

⅔ cup dark brown sugar, sieved to remove any lumps

½ teaspoon baking powder

½ cup orange marmalade

⅓ cup honey

2 teaspoons baking soda

1 cup milk

Preheat the oven to 325°. Grease a 6-cup loaf pan with the butter. Dust it with some flour, tapping out the excess. Set the pan aside.

Put the flour, brown sugar, and baking powder in a large bowl and mix together. Put the marmalade and honey in a large bowl. Dissolve the baking soda in the milk and stir it into the marmalade and honey. Add the flour mixture to the marmalade mixture and stir until the batter is well mixed.

Pour the batter into the prepared pan and bake until the pain d'épice crowns on top and a wooden skewer inserted in the center of the cake comes out clean, about 1 hour.

Let it cool to room temperature in the pan on a rack, then tip the loaf out of the pan. Serve it sliced, and slathered with butter, if you like.

GOLDEN FRUITCAKE
makes 2 cakes

This is more fruit than cake, and a little slice goes a long way!

1½ cups sliced almonds, toasted
¾ cup candied lemon peel, minced
¾ cup candied orange peel, minced
1 cup golden raisins
1 cup dried apricots, minced
1 cup candied ginger, minced
1 apple, peeled, cored, and grated on the large holes of a box grater
1 cup orange liqueur
½ pound plus 3 tablespoons (19 tablespoons) unsalted butter, softened

1 cup flour
1 teaspoon baking soda
1 teaspoon ground mace
½ teaspoon salt
¼ teaspoon ground cloves
1 cup dried fine white bread crumbs
1 cup sugar
4 eggs
½ cup sour cream
½ cup fresh lemon juice
2 tablespoons vanilla extract
Cognac or brandy

Combine the almonds, candied citrus peel, raisins, apricots, ginger, apple, and orange liqueur in a bowl. Set aside. Let macerate at room temperature overnight.

Preheat oven to 350°. Grease two fluted 4-cup tube pans with 2 tablespoons of the butter and set aside. Sift or whisk the flour, baking soda, mace, salt, and cloves together in another mixing bowl. Stir in the bread crumbs and set aside.

Beat 16 tablespoons of the butter in a large bowl with an electric mixer on medium speed, gradually adding the sugar and beating until the butter is light and fluffy. Beat in eggs one at a time, then beat in the sour cream, lemon juice, and vanilla. Gradually add the flour mixture, mixing until well combined. Use a rubber spatula to gently fold in the macerated fruit and liquid.

Divide the batter between the prepared pans. Grease 2 sheets of foil with the remaining 1 tablespoon butter then cover the tube pans with it. Set the tube pans into a deep roasting pan. Add enough hot water to come one-third up the sides of the tube pans. Bake the fruitcakes until a toothpick inserted in the center comes out clean, about 1 hour and 45 minutes.

Unmold warm cakes onto a rack. They are ready to serve. If you like them a little boozy, sprinkle them with a little Cognac each day for a week. Wrap in plastic and refrigerate. Unwrap them each day to give them a little drink.

THANKSGIVING

❧ HAPPY THANKSGIVING ❧

Hot Spiked Cider ❧ French Cheese Puffs

Shrimp and Pickled Celery

Pumpkin Soup with Pimentón and Preserved Lemon
or
Triple X Chicken Broth with Ricotta Ravioli

Neenie's Sourdough-Sage Stuffing
or
Chestnut Stuffing

Roast Capon with Fettuccine Stuffing
or
Roast Turkey

Glazed Carrots
❧
Brian's Mashed Potato Trick
❧
Creamed Onions

Cranberry Port Gelée

Sweet Potato Pie ❧ Agee's Pecan Pie

HOT SPIKED CIDER
serves 8–10

This is less a recipe than a reminder that a pot of simmering cider on the stove fills the kitchen with the fragrance of fall.

2 quarts apple cider
Cinnamon sticks

1½ cups Calvados or brandy, optional

Put the cider and 1 cinnamon stick into a pot and bring to a simmer over medium-low heat. Reduce heat to low to keep cider warm. Ladle the hot cider into mugs and add the booze if you want to. Add a cinnamon stick to each.

FRENCH CHEESE PUFFS
makes about 3 dozen

Every time we serve these beauties the crowd goes wild. They are the perfect appetizer—flavorful, crisp, and delicate.

8 tablespoons butter
1¼ cups milk
2 pinches salt
Pepper

1 cup flour
4 large eggs
1 cup grated Comté or
   Gruyère cheese

Preheat oven to 400°. Put the butter and 1 cup of the milk into a medium, heavy-bottomed saucepan and season with salt and a few grinds of pepper. Heat over medium heat until milk is hot and the butter has melted, about 5 minutes.

Reduce heat to low. Add all of the flour at once and stir vigorously with a wooden spoon until the dough forms a thick mass and pulls away from sides of the pan.

Remove pan from the heat and beat in the eggs, one at a time, beating vigorously with the wooden spoon until each egg is absorbed into dough before adding the next. The dough should be thick, smooth, and shiny. Beat in the cheese.

Spoon small spoonfuls of dough (about the size of a walnut) onto nonstick or parchment paper-lined baking sheets, about 1 inch apart. Brush tops with some of the remaining milk (this will give the cheese puffs a nice shiny top). Bake until puffed and golden brown, about 20 minutes. Serve warm.

SHRIMP AND PICKLED CELERY
serves 8

Most of the time celery is appreciated for its crunch; but it is delicious when poached into tender suppleness.

FOR THE PICKLING BRINE
1 cup rice wine vinegar
1 cup mirin
¼ cup sugar
3 thick slices fresh ginger
10 black peppercorns
2 cinnamon sticks
10 juniper berries

4 whole celery hearts, some leaves reserved for garnish
1 cup white wine
8 black peppercorns
2 bay leaves
Salt and pepper
24–32 medium unpeeled shrimp
Really good extra-virgin olive oil
1 lemon, cut into 8 wedges

For the pickling brine, mix all of the ingredients together along with 1 cup water in a pot and cook over medium heat, stirring from time to time, until the sugar has dissolved. Pour the pickling brine into a wide shallow dish. This brine can be made up to a week before using. Keep refrigerated.

Remove any large ribs of celery from the hearts. Keep the hearts whole. Put the hearts into a large pot with just enough water to cover. Add the wine, peppercorns, bay leaves, and a generous pinch of salt. Cover and simmer over medium heat until the celery is very tender when pierced with a paring knife, about 45 minutes. Use tongs to remove the hearts from the pot, taking care to keep them whole. Transfer the celery to the pickling brine.

Using the same pot and water in which you cooked the celery, poach the shrimp until just cooked, about 3 minutes. Drain, then peel and devein the shrimp. Add the shrimp to the celery in the poaching liquid. Make sure everything is submerged. If there isn't enough brine to cover everything completely just give the celery and shrimp a turn every now and then. Cover with plastic wrap, refrigerate, and allow shrimp and celery to "pickle" for about an hour.

Use a sharp knife to halve the celery lengthwise. Place half a celery heart on each of 8 plates. Arrange 3 or 4 shrimp on top of the celery. Drizzle with olive oil, season with salt and pepper, and garnish with celery leaves and a lemon wedge.

PUMPKIN SOUP WITH PIMENTÓN AND PRESERVED LEMON
serves about 8

A Canal House lunch was planned for the illustrious Chez Panisse chef, David Tanis (*A Platter of Figs*, Artisan Books, 2008). We decided on a first course of pumpkin soup using the very pumpkins themselves as the "soup pots". It would take four pumpkins to feed twenty people. We would flavor the flesh with smoky pimentón and preserved lemons, add chicken broth, then roast them in the oven. The four pumpkins would be placed down the middle of the table with a big tah-dah, the lids lifted by the stems, the aromatic steam rising, and the guests would ladle the succulent pumpkin and broth into their own bowls. We put the word out and heard tell that a nearby farm had grown the pumpkin of all pumpkins, so we couldn't resist. Melissa hopped in the car and roared off to fetch it. Forty-five minutes later she called and asked me to come downstairs and help her carry the prize up into the studio. Now Melissa has great pride in her amazing strength and I have seen her sling a large dressed lamb over her shoulder without turning a hair, so frankly I was surprised at her request for help. Then I saw it—a Rouge Vif d'Etampes pumpkin so big that Cinderella could indeed have used it for her coach. It must have weighed thirty-five pounds. So 4 pumpkin soups became one big pumpkin soup! But the dang thing wouldn't even fit in our oven so we hauled it to a nearby restaurant and roasted it there. Quite a sight it was parading back and forth down the street. All the heavy lifting was worth it though—it was a beauty of a soup and our guests loved it. Someone said it was the most delicious thing she had ever eaten in her life. Aw, shucks. —— CH

It is important to use a variety of pumpkin that is sturdy and won't collapse during roasting, like the thick-fleshed Rouge Vif d'Etampes, Cinderella, or Cheese.

Preheat oven to 350°. Cut out a lid around the stem-end of an 8–10 pound Rouge Vif d'Etampes pumpkin and set aside. Scrape out and discard the seeds and strings. Put pumpkin on a baking sheet along with the lid. Rub the pumpkin flesh with lots of softened butter. Rub in coarse salt and pepper, and 2 tablespoons pimentón. Add the finely chopped rinds of 2 preserved lemons, a couple of sliced garlic cloves and 2 bay leaves. Fill the pumpkin halfway full with a good broth like Triple X Chicken Broth, opposite page. Roast until flesh is soft when pierced with a paring knife. Take care not to puncture the skin. Replace lid for effect, if you like, and serve the pumpkin soup at the table, scraping the flesh from the bottom and sides into the broth then ladling it into bowls.

TRIPLE X CHICKEN BROTH WITH RICOTTA RAVIOLI
serves 8–12

Make the broth well ahead of your holiday meal then all you have to do is reheat the broth, boil the pasta, and assemble. The cooked buttered ravioli can sit for an hour. The hot broth will heat them up. If you have the time to make your favorite homemade ravioli, by all means it will be well worth it. But we endorse finding a good fresh store-bought ravioli; you just might have time to take a walk or better yet a Thanksgiving nap—build up your appetite.

6 pounds chicken wings
3 stalks celery, chopped
1 smoked ham hock
2 carrots, peeled and chopped
1 large yellow onion, chopped
1 bottle dry white wine

Half a bunch of parsley
2 bay leaves
10 black peppercorns
Salt and pepper
About 36 small ricotta ravioli
4 tablespoons butter

Put the chicken wings, celery, ham hock, carrots, onions, wine, parsley, bay leaves, and peppercorns into a large heavy pot. Add 1 gallon (16 cups) water. Bring to a boil over medium-high heat. Allow it to boil for about 10 minutes then reduce the heat to low. Gently simmer (just barely bubbling), uncovered, for about 4 hours. The broth should reduce by half. Remove and reserve the ham hock. Strain the broth through a fine sieve and discard the solids. Return the broth to the pot. Season with salt and pepper. Don't skim off the fat, it will add a delicious richness to the broth. Cover and keep warm over very low heat. (If you are making the broth ahead, allow it to cool to room temperature, then cover and refrigerate or freeze it.)

Remove the meat from the ham hock; discard the bones and gristle. Finely chop the meat. Keep well wrapped until just before serving.

Cook the ravioli in a large pot of boiling salted water over medium-high heat until they float to the surface. Drain in a colander. Melt the butter in the same hot pot off the heat, then return the drained ravioli to the pot, shaking the pot to coat the pasta in the melted butter. Season with salt and pepper.

Divide the minced ham hock meat between the soup bowls. Divide the ravioli between the bowls, arranging them on top of the ham. Ladle the hot broth over the ravioli. Serve with grated parmigiano-reggiano, if you like.

NEENIE'S SOURDOUGH-SAGE STUFFING
serves about 12

Every year, about three days before Thanksgiving, my great-aunt Cele would deliver three large loaves of Boudin sourdough bread to my grandmother's San Francisco apartment. It was the first sign that Thanksgiving preparations had begun. The giant loaves would be split open, their crisp crusts cracking as the serrated knife sawed them in half. Neenie (the childish name that a grandchild had christened her) would sit on one of her delicate upholstered side chairs with a TV tray next to her piled high with bread. She would spread a diaphanous white flour-sack dish towel over her lap, then pick tiny crumbs from the bread while watching her stories, *Another World* and *The Guiding Light*. She prided herself on the fineness of the crumb. I hope that I can live up to her standards. —— CH

½ pound (16 tablespoons) butter
3 medium yellow onions, finely chopped
1 head celery, finely chopped
1 large bunch parsley, leaves finely chopped

6 large sprigs fresh sage, leaves finely chopped
Salt and pepper
10 cups fine, fresh sourdough bread crumbs
½ cup chicken stock

Melt the butter in a large heavy-bottomed skillet over medium-low heat. Add the onions and cook, stirring occasionally, until they are very soft and translucent and haven't taken on any color, about 20 minutes. Add the celery, parsley, and sage and season with salt and pepper. Cook for 5 minutes. Transfer to a large mixing bowl.

Add the bread crumbs to the bowl with the onions and celery and toss until well combined. Stir in the chicken stock, mixing until the stuffing is moist but not packed together or dense. Adjust the seasoning.

Spoon the stuffing into a turkey (see page 84 for a roast turkey recipe) and roast. Or, put the stuffing into a large buttered baking dish and bake in a preheated 325° oven until it is hot throughout and golden on top, about 45 minutes.

VARIATION: To stuff a capon or a large roaster with Neenie's Sourdough-Sage Stuffing, reduce the recipe by half and use it in place of the Fettuccine Stuffing recipe (see page 82) spooning it into the bird, then roast it.

CHESTNUT STUFFING
serves about 12

We're cooks who have endless patience for "process." But when the recipe calls for 5 cups of peeled chestnuts, which means hours of scoring their tough skins with x's, roasting them, peeling them while they are still hot, then dealing with those fuzzy inner skins—life is too short. We cut ourselves some slack and reach for jars of those nice French already peeled chestnuts. Their flavor is just fine.

5 cups peeled chestnuts

½ cup vin santo, sherry, Madeira, or other sweet or fortified wine

½ pound (16 tablespoons) butter

1 medium yellow onion, chopped

5 cups coarse fresh bread crumbs

Leaves of 2–3 large sprigs fresh thyme

2 handfuls fresh parsley leaves, finely chopped

Salt and pepper

1–1½ cups chicken stock

Put the chestnuts in a large wide bowl, sprinkle with the wine, and set aside.

Melt the butter in a large skillet over medium heat. Add the onions and cook, stirring often, until they are soft, about 5 minutes. Add the bread crumbs and thyme, and cook, stirring from time to time, until golden, about 10 minutes. Transfer the bread crumbs to the bowl with the chestnuts. Add the parsley and season with salt and pepper. Mix the stuffing with your hands, breaking about half of the chestnuts into large pieces.

Stir the chicken stock into the stuffing, mixing in just enough to moisten it without making it packed or dense.

Spoon the stuffing into a turkey, (see page 84 for a roast turkey recipe) and roast. Or, put the stuffing into a large buttered baking dish and bake in a preheated 325° oven, covered, for 30 minutes. Uncover and bake until golden on top, 15–20 minutes more.

VARIATION: To stuff a capon or a large roasting chicken with Chestnut Stuffing, reduce the recipe by half and use it in place of the Fettuccine Stuffing recipe (see page 82), spooning it into the bird, then roast it.

ROAST CAPON WITH FETTUCCINE STUFFING
serves 6–8

My mother isn't a fan of turkey (too big, dry as sawdust, and tasteless are her sentiments regarding the bird). So we grew up eating roast capon for our Thanksgiving dinner. I don't remember if she even stuffed it. It was just the right size of big, always juicy, and we loved the flavor. So life goes on and times change, and now it's my father who takes on the Thanksgiving holiday meal. Sometimes he'll roast a turkey (he's into boning them out and stuffing them these days), but my favorite is when he makes roast capon with this unusual stuffing. It really has it all—the traditional and the unconventional. Just like my family. —— MH

FOR THE STUFFING
½ cup dried wild mushrooms,
  preferably porcini
3 tablespoons butter
2 chicken livers, trimmed
6 fresh mushrooms, sliced
  (most any kind will do, but
  not portobellos)
Leaves of 3–4 sprigs fresh thyme
2–3 pinches cayenne

Salt and pepper
½ cup finely diced baked ham
Handful fresh parsley leaves,
  chopped
¾ pound fettuccine

One 7–8 pound capon
3 tablespoons butter, softened
Salt and pepper

For the stuffing, put the dried mushrooms into a small bowl, cover with boiling water, and soak until soft, about 10 minutes. Lift the mushrooms from the soaking liquid and rinse them if they are gritty. Chop the mushrooms and put them into a large bowl. Bring a large pot of salted water to a boil.

Meanwhile, melt the butter in a medium skillet over medium-high heat. Add the chicken livers and sauté until browned, 3–5 minutes. Remove them from the skillet and set aside. Add the fresh mushrooms, thyme, and cayenne to the skillet, season with salt and pepper, and sauté until browned, about 5 minutes. Add the mushrooms to the bowl with the wild mushrooms. Chop the sautéed chicken livers and add them to the bowl. Add the ham and parsley and mix well.

continued

Cook the fettuccine in the pot of boiling water over high heat until it is just tender, about 8 minutes. Drain the pasta and toss it with the mushroom mixture. Taste the stuffing and adjust the seasoning.

Preheat the oven to 350°. Rub the capon all over with the butter and season it inside and out with salt and pepper. Spoon the stuffing into capon cavity. Tie the legs together with kitchen string.

Put the capon on a rack set inside a large roasting pan. Add 1 cup of water to the pan. Roast the capon, basting it occasionally with the pan juices, until it is golden brown and the internal temperature of the thigh registers 165°, about 2 hours.

Transfer the capon to a serving platter and let it rest for about 20 minutes. Serve the capon and stuffing with the pan juices.

ROAST TURKEY
serves 10–16

We've cooked turkeys every which way: in a brown grocery bag (turns out to be highly unsanitary), draped with butter-drenched cheesecloth, deep fried, deboned and shaped into a melon (oh la la!), we even wrestled with a hot twenty-five pounder, turning it breast side down, then breast side up, and on and on. But we think we've found the answer to our annual quest for moist tender turkey. Judy Rogers, in her award-winning tome, *The Zuni Cafe Cookbook* (Norton, 2002), taught us all about the benefits of dry-brining pork and chicken. Russ Parsons, the food editor and columnist for the *L.A. Times*, applied Judy's technique to achieving the perfect Thanksgiving turkey. Here's our version of Russ' recipe.

Rinse a 14–16-pound fresh turkey (not injected or pre-brined) and pat dry with paper towels. Rub or pat 3 tablespoons kosher salt onto the breasts, legs, and thighs. Tightly wrap the turkey completely in plastic wrap or slip it into a very large resealable plastic bag, pressing out the air before sealing it. Set the turkey on a pan breast side up and refrigerate it for 3 days. Turn the turkey every day, massaging the salt into the skin through the plastic.

Unwrap the turkey and pat it dry with paper towels (don't rinse the bird). Return the turkey to the pan breast side up and refrigerate it, uncovered, for at least 8 hours or overnight.

Remove the turkey from the refrigerator and let it come to room temperature, at least 1 hour. Preheat the oven to 325°.

If you've decided to serve your turkey stuffed, spoon the stuffing of your choice (see pages 80 through 83 for some of our favorites) into the cavity of the bird. (Put any extra stuffing into a buttered baking dish, cover, and put it in the oven to bake with the turkey for the last hour.) Tie the legs together with kitchen string. Tuck the wings under the back. Rub the turkey all over with 3–4 tablespoons softened butter. Place the turkey breast side up on a roasting rack set into a large roasting pan. Add 1 cup water to the pan. Roast the turkey until it is golden brown and a thermometer inserted into the thigh registers 165°, about 3 hours for an unstuffed bird and 3–4 hours for a stuffed one.

Transfer the turkey to a platter, loosely cover it with foil, and let it rest for 20–30 minutes before carving. Serve the turkey and stuffing, if using, with the pan drippings.

GLAZED CARROTS
serves 8

Cut 3 pounds peeled young carrots into large pieces. Put the carrots, 3 tablespoons butter, 3 tablespoons dark brown sugar, ¼ cup sherry, and salt and pepper into a medium, heavy-bottomed pot. Cover and cook over medium heat until the carrots are just tender, about 20 minutes. Uncover and continue to cook until the sauce reduces a bit, about 10 minutes. Serve with a little chopped parsley, if you like.

BRIAN'S MASHED POTATO TRICK

Brian Beadle is my son-in-law. This great big guy is kind of a finicky eater—he's a meat and potatoes man. You could say he is sort of a specialist so we leave the spud-making to him. His mashed potato recipe is fairly standard. But his trick is to slip tiny pats of cold butter down into and throughout the hot potatoes when they are in their serving dish. The butter melts into hidden pools buried deep in the mashed potatoes to be discovered with each delicious forkful. —— CH

CREAMED ONIONS
makes as many as you have the patience to peel

The hardest part of these creamed onions is peeling them. But don't be tempted to use frozen peeled onions, they are watery and a little sour.

Bring a large pot of salted water to a boil over high heat. Plunge white or yellow pearl onions into the water for a minute. Scoop out the onions with a sieve. When they are cool enough to handle, use a paring knife to cut off the root end, then pop the onions out of their skins. Put the peeled onions into a gratin dish and pour in equal parts of whole milk and heavy cream to just cover the onions. Baked in a preheated 325° oven until onions are tender and the cream has thickened, about 30 minutes. Remove the onions from the oven, season with salt and pepper, and a good grating of nutmeg. Increase the heat to 400° then return the dish to the oven and cook until bubbling and golden, about 10 minutes more.

CRANBERRY PORT GELÉE
makes about 2 cups

Use a good port or red wine or even a Madeira if that's what you have on hand. Cranberries have so much natural pectin that this sauce will set up even if you don't refrigerate it.

I cup port
I cup sugar
I tablespoon juniper berries

10 black peppercorns
4 cups or I bag fresh cranberries

Put the port, sugar, juniper berries, and peppercorns into a heavy saucepan and bring to a boil over medium-high heat. Add the cranberries and return to a boil. Reduce the heat to low and simmer until the cranberries burst and are very soft, about 10 minutes more.

Strain the sauce into a bowl through a fine-mesh sieve, pushing the solids through the screen with a rubber spatula. Transfer to a pretty serving bowl. Cover and refrigerate.

ODE TO CRANBERRY SAUCE

You simply have to have cranberry sauce with roast turkey and gravy. Its tart fruity zing slides right underneath the taste of a forkful of gravy-drenched turkey and lifts it up to a higher place. We love our recipe above, but we also love the recipe on the back of the bag of Ocean Spray cranberries. It always works! Just boil 1 cup sugar, 1 cup water, and a bag of cranberries in a pot over high heat. Reduce the heat to medium and cook until the berries burst. Strain it or leave in the berries for a gutsier sauce. Don't forget to add it to your turkey sandwich the next day. After all, isn't that the whole point of roasting the turkey—to get to the moment of eating a mayo and cranberry sauce-slathered turkey sandwich on white bread?

Sweet Potato Pie

SWEET POTATO PIE
makes one 9-inch pie

The flesh of the sweet potato is so dense and meaty that you only need a sliver of this pie to feel satisfied. It is the perfect final act of Thanksgiving dinner.

FOR THE FILLING
4–6 sweet potatoes, to make about
  2½ cups of roasted flesh
½ cup molasses or sorghum
3 egg yolks
1 teaspoon ground ginger
1 teaspoon ground cinnamon
1 teaspoon ground mace

FOR THE CRUST
1½ cups flour
Salt
10 tablespoons cold unsalted butter,
  cut into small pieces

Freshly whipped cream

For the filling, preheat the oven to 375°. Bake the sweet potatoes until tender, about 1 hour. Remove from the oven, set aside, and allow to cool.

For the pie crust, while the sweet potatoes bake, whisk the flour and a pinch of salt in a large mixing bowl. Blend in the butter with a pasty blender or a fork until crumbly. It should resemble coarse cornmeal. Sprinkle in 5 tablespoons ice water and toss lightly; form into a ball. Don't overhandle. Wrap dough in plastic wrap and chill for at least an hour.

When the potatoes are cool enough to handle, scoop out the flesh into a large bowl. Discard the skins. Add the molasses, egg yolks, and spices, and mix together well.

Roll out the dough into an 12-inch round on a lightly floured surface. Roll dough loosely around the rolling pin and place into a 9-inch pie pan. Lightly press it into the pan. Leave 1 inch of dough hanging over the edge and trim any extra off with a sharp knife. Tuck the dough under itself, then use your thumb and forefinger to crimp the edge.

Pour the filling into the unbaked pie shell and smooth the top with a rubber spatula. Bake for 45 minutes. Serve with whipped cream.

AGEE'S PECAN PIE
makes two 8-inch pies

Afra Lineberry, Agee to her family, opened The Jerre Anne Bake Shoppe in St. Joe, Missouri, in 1930. It was the last stop on the trolley line. Conductors would leave their cars running while they ran into Agee's for a cup of coffee and a piece of pie. "It seems like I just always knew how to make a good pie crust. It may take a little practice for some, but the only time to get excited about a pie crust is when you're eating it," Agee used to say. The little shop grew to be a smashing success, and by 1990, with Geraldine Lawhon (Agee's niece) running the shop, they were selling 625 pies at Thanksgiving alone. Sadly, the Jerre Anne closed its doors in 2008. When you eat Agee's pie, send your thanks heavenward.

FOR THE PIE CRUST
1½ cups flour
½ teaspoon salt
6 tablespoons cold vegetable
   shortening
2 tablespoons cold lard

FOR THE PECAN FILLING
1½ cups light corn syrup
5 tablespoons butter, melted
1 cup light brown sugar (not packed)
Pinch of salt
¼ teaspoon vanilla extract
4 eggs, beaten
2 cups pecan halves (not pieces)

For the pie crust, whisk together flour and salt in a bowl. Blend in shortening and lard with a pasty blender or a fork until crumbly. It should resemble fine pieces of grain. Sprinkle with ¼ cup ice water and toss lightly. Form into a ball. Don't overhandle. Wrap dough in plastic wrap and chill for at least an hour.

Roll out half the dough on a lightly floured surface into an ⅛-inch thick round. Roll dough loosely around the rolling pin and place in an 8-inch pie tin. Lightly press dough into the tin. Trim the excess dough from the edge with a sharp knife. Use your thumb and forefinger to crimp edges. Repeat with remaining dough.

For the pecan filling, preheat oven to 350°. Mix together the corn syrup, melted butter, and brown sugar in a large bowl until sugar has dissolved. Add the salt, vanilla, and eggs, mixing well after each addition.

Arrange 1 cup of the pecans right side up in each unbaked pie shell, then gently pour in the filling. The pecans will float to the top. Bake for 45–50 minutes or until a knife inserted in the middle comes out clean. Cool to room temperature.

the holidays

seven beautiful fishes

LA VIGILIA ✤ CHRISTMAS EVE

La Vigilia, the Feast of the Seven Fishes, is the traditional Southern Italian Christmas Eve dinner. The day before Christmas is a day of abstinence for Roman Catholics, so no meat may be consumed. You can imagine how the Italians, with all their beautiful fish preparations, twirl this religious exercise of self-denial into one of delicious indulgence. The meal will sometimes expand beyond the traditional seven different dishes made with fish and sea-food. We used the number seven as a guide, and, playing by American rules, mixed and matched our cuisines. What a great night before Christmas.

WHOLE FISH BAKED ON POTATOES
serves 6

We like to arrange the potatoes in the pan so they overlap slightly to resemble fish scales, but it is not necessary. Just be sure they are in a thin layer so they cook evenly by the time the fish is done.

½ cup extra-virgin olive oil
12 medium all-purpose white
  potatoes, peeled and thinly sliced
1 small yellow onion, thinly sliced

Salt and pepper
One whole 2-pound flounder,
  cleaned
¼ cup dry white wine

Preheat the oven to 375°. Pour a thin film of the olive oil into a roasting pan large enough so the fish can lay flat in it. Arrange the potatoes in the bottom of the pan in a single layer, slightly overlapping. The potatoes should cover the bottom of the pan. Arrange the onions over the potatoes, then drizzle with 2–3 tablespoons oil. Season with salt and pepper. Put the pan in the oven and bake the potatoes until they begin to brown around the edges of the pan, about 20 minutes.

Remove the pan from the oven. Lay the fish on top of the potatoes belly side down. Splash the wine over the fish and potatoes and drizzle with the remaining oil. Season with salt and pepper. Return the pan to the oven and bake until the potatoes are tender and the fish is just cooked through, about 20 minutes.

Let the fish rest for 5 or 10 minutes, then peel off the skin and fillet it. Serve with the potatoes.

WHITE ASPARAGUS WITH ANCHOVY VINAIGRETTE
serves 6

The Spanish are masters of jarred vegetables, and one of our favorites is the white asparagus from the Navarra region. We don't find them everywhere so we always grab a few jars when we are in stores that carry them.

Put 1 small clove garlic, one drained 4-ounce jar anchovies packed in oil, and 1 cup good extra-virgin olive oil into a food processor and blend until smooth. Transfer to a container. (It will keep for up to 2 weeks in the refrigerator.) Drain 2 jars of Spanish white asparagus and arrange them on a serving platter. Spoon some vinaigrette over the asparagus. Garnish with chives.

BROILED MUSSELS
serves 6

Slip these mussels into a 500° oven to bake if you don't have a broiler.

Put 2 pounds cleaned mussels and ½ cup white wine into a medium pot, cover, and steam them open over high heat, about 5 minutes. Set aside to cool completely. Twist off and discard one of the shells from each mussel (discard any unopened mussels), making sure that the remaining shell has a mussel in it. Reserve the mussel broth for another use. Put 4 tablespoons softened butter, 1 handful chopped fresh parsley leaves, 1 small clove minced garlic, 4 pinches pimentón, and salt to taste into a bowl and mash together into a paste. Slather each mussel in its shell with some of the seasoned butter and arrange on a shallow baking or broiler pan. Refrigerate the mussels until the butter is hard. Preheat the broiler. Broil the mussels until the butter is bubbling hot, about 2 minutes.

POACHED OYSTERS WITH LEMON
serves 6

Shuck your own oysters or buy a tub of already shucked ones for this appetizer.

Put 1 bay leaf, a few black peppercorns, half of a preserved lemon, ¼ cup red wine vinegar, and 1 cup extra-virgin olive oil into a medium pan. Gently heat over medium-low heat until warm. Add a dozen or so shucked plump oysters and gently poach them until they are just barely firm, 2–3 minutes depending on the size of the oysters. Transfer the oysters and poaching liquid to a dish and let come to room temperature. Serve with club crackers or little toasts.

LOBSTER STEW
serves 4–6

At Christmas, sometimes you are shopping up to the last minute. Give yourself a gift and order your lobster ahead. When you do, ask your fishmarket to steam and crack the lobsters for you just before you pick them up and if they have good fish stock, pick that up, too.

Two 1½-pound lobsters
Salt
4 tablespoons butter
1 yellow onion, finely chopped
2 ribs celery, diced
2 sprigs fresh tarragon

Pepper
2–3 russet potatoes, peeled and diced
1 cup white wine
1 cup good fish stock
1 cup heavy cream
Chopped chives for garnish

Plunge the tip of a large sharp knife into the heads of the lobsters just behind the eyes. (This is the hardest part of the whole recipe.) Drop the lobsters into a large pot of salted boiling water over high heat and cook for about 8 minutes. Remove the lobsters from the pot and set them aside until they are cool enough to handle.

Remove the meat from the lobster, reserving the shells and any juices. Cut the lobster into large bite-size pieces, leaving the claw meat whole.

Melt the butter in a large heavy pot over medium-low heat. Add onions, celery, and tarragon. Season with salt and pepper. Add the large pieces of lobster shells along with any juices and cook, stirring from time to time, for 10 minutes. Add potatoes, wine, and fish stock, cover, and gently simmer until the vegetables are just soft, about 15 minutes. Remove and discard the tarragon and lobster shells.

Add cream and lobster meat and cook until lobster is just heated through, about 5 minutes. Taste for seasoning. Ladle into bowls; garnish with chives.

BRANDADE
serves 6

Our local supermarket sells salt cod in little boxes and also loose in a bin. We prefer to chose our own from the bin. That way we get the fattest pieces.

½ pound salt cod
2 russet potatoes, peeled and diced
2 cloves garlic, crushed
½ cup whole milk, warmed

Extra-virgin olive oil
Salt and pepper
Little toasts

Soak the salt cod in a large bowl of cold water in the refrigerator or a cool place for 2 days, changing the water a couple times a day.

Preheat the oven to 350°. Drain the fish and cut it into large pieces. Put the fish into a medium pot, cover with cold water, and bring to a simmer over medium heat. Reduce the heat to low and gently simmer until the fish flakes easily, about 15 minutes. Drain and set aside until cool enough to handle. Remove and discard any skin and bones from the fish. Set the fish aside.

Put the potatoes and garlic into a medium pot of cold water and boil over medium heat until the potatoes are soft, 10–15 minutes. Drain and set aside.

Put the fish, potatoes, garlic, milk, and a good splash of olive oil into a food processor and process until fairly smooth. Season to taste with a little salt and pepper. Spoon the brandade into a small baking dish. Drizzle with some olive oil and bake until golden on top, about 20 minutes. Serve with little toasts.

LANGOUSTINE LACE
serves 6

Use either small langoustine or bay shrimp to make these crispy little appetizers.

Whisk ½ cup flour, 2 large pinches of salt, and 1 cup white wine in a medium bowl until smooth. Stir 1 pound chopped peeled langoustine into the batter. Add enough vegetable oil to a cast iron skillet to reach a depth of 2 inches. Heat over medium heat until hot. Slide small forkfuls of the langoustine batter into the oil and fry the little fritters until lightly golden, about 1 minute. Drain on paper towels. Season with salt while still hot. Garnish with chopped parsley.

CHRISTMAS DINNERS

HOT TODDY
makes 4

My husband has taken to making these warm, comforting drinks during the Christmas season. It's a cross between a hot buttered rum and a hot toddy—the best of both worlds. Practical man that he is, he keeps a big batch of the spiced butter in the fridge ready to go all season long. —— MH

4 tablespoons salted butter, softened
2 tablespoons dark brown sugar
2–3 pinches ground cinnamon

2–3 pinches ground nutmeg
2–3 pinches ground cloves
8 ounces bourbon or dark rum

Mix the butter, sugar, cinnamon, nutmeg, and cloves together in a small bowl. Divide the spiced butter between four cups or mugs. Add 2 ounces of the bourbon or rum to each cup and stir in boiling water. Top the drink with a dash of cinnamon or nutmeg.

MILK PUNCH
serves 8

We make this frosty deliciousness by the pitcherful, letting it get nice and icy in the freezer just before serving it.

1 quart whole milk
1 cup half-and-half
1½ cups bourbon, whiskey,
  or brandy

1 cup powdered sugar, sifted
1 tablespoon vanilla extract
Ground nutmeg

Put the milk, half-and-half, booze, sugar, and vanilla extract into a pitcher and stir well. Put the pitcher into the freezer and chill the milk punch until it is quite slushy, 3–4 hours. Stir well and serve in pretty chilled glasses, garnished with a dash of nutmeg.

THE FISHERMAN'S WIFE'S GRAVLAX
makes enough for a crowd

In the days of big fat expense accounts, when PR companies were wining and dining the press, I was invited on a Norwegian Salmon press trip. This was a very very fancy trip! We traveled through France and ate salmon prepared by the finest chefs starting at Taillevent in Paris and ending up in the hands of Roger Vergé at Le Moulin de Mougins on the Riviera. Finally, we flew to Norway where the King of Norway's chef, no less, prepared salmon with cloudberries for us. But the most delicious salmon of all was gravlax made by the wife of a salmon fisherman on a tiny, beautifully stark island in the wild North Sea. I wrote down the recipe and make it every year at Christmas. —— CH

1 whole salmon, 5–6 pounds, filleted
  into two halves
¼ cup coarse salt
2 tablespoons sugar
3 tablespoons coarsely ground
  white pepper
⅓ cup finely chopped fresh dill leaves
¼ cup aquavit or Cognac

FOR THE MUSTARD SAUCE
2 big tablespoons honey mustard
1 tablespoon fresh lemon juice or
  white wine vinegar
¼ cup canola oil
1 tablespoon finely chopped chives
1 tablespoon finely chopped fresh dill
  or fennel fronds

To cure the salmon, mix together salt, sugar, pepper, and dill in a bowl. Lay the salmon halves skin side down on a work surface. Divide the salt evenly between both halves and rub it into the salmon flesh. Sprinkle aquavit over the salmon. Place one half of salmon, flesh side up, in a large, shallow pan so that it lays flat. Lay the other salmon half on top, skin side up, head to tail (a flesh-to-flesh salmon sandwich). Press a large sheet of plastic wrap directly onto the fish to seal it from the air. Put it in an accessible spot in your fridge, then place a cookie sheet or a pan of similar size on top of fish and weight with heavy cans. This will press out any liquid and give the gravlax a firm silky texture. Turn fish over a couple of times each day (once a day will do if you are very busy), and baste it with the juices.

After 5 days, the salmon will be cured. Remove salmon from the pan and wipe off any salt and herbs. Thinly slice salmon from the skin and arrange slices on a platter. Serve with bread, fresh chives, lemons, and mustard sauce. Refrigerate well-wrapped gravlax for up to one week.

For the mustard sauce, whisk together all the ingredients in a bowl.

ROAST PRIME RIB OF BEEF
serves 8–10

We favor roasting large cuts of meat at a low temperature; the gentle heat cooks them evenly throughout (which means beautifully rosy pink slices of beef).

1 8–12-pound prime rib roast of beef, tied between the ribs
Salt and pepper

Preheat oven to 200°. Generously season roast all over with salt and pepper. Heat a heavy skillet large enough to accommodate the roast and sear the meaty sides of the roast until nicely browned, 5–10 minutes.

Transfer the roast to a large roasting pan, rib side down, and roast in the oven until the internal temperature reaches 120° for rare, 130°–135° for medium-rare, and 140° for medium, 3–4½ hours.

Transfer the roast beef to a carving board or a warm serving platter and let it rest for 30 minutes. Remove string before carving the roast.

LITTLE YORKSHIRE PUDDINGS
makes 8

Use the pan drippings from the roast beef for best flavor.

1 cup flour
½ teaspoon salt
2 eggs, lightly beaten

1 cup whole milk
3–4 tablespoons roast beef pan
    drippings or melted butter

Whisk together flour and salt in a medium bowl. Add eggs and milk, whisking until batter is well mixed (it's okay if there are a few lumps). Cover and refrigerate the batter for at least 1 hour or as long as overnight.

Preheat oven to 425°. Put a small spoonful of pan drippings or butter into each cup of an 8-mold popover or muffin pan and put pan into the oven until it is hot. Give batter a stir then pour it into hot cups, filling them no more than three-quarters full. Quickly return pan to oven and bake for 15 minutes. Reduce heat to 350° and continue baking until puffed and browned, about 20 minutes more (resist the urge to open the oven door and peek; the puddings will deflate). Tip puddings out of cups and poke their sides with a toothpick to let steam escape. Serve hot.

Left, Crown Roast of Pork with Corn Bread Stuffing; above, Baked Apples with Savory Stuffing

CROWN ROAST OF PORK WITH CORN BREAD STUFFING
serves 10–14

This majestic pork roast is composed of two center-cut rib roasts that are tied together rib sides out into the shape of a crown. We always ask our butcher for a pound of ground pork for the stuffing to fill the center of the crown. Be sure to order your crown roast from your butcher ahead of time and request the ribs "frenched"—cleaned of meat and sinew—for a more elegant presentation.

FOR THE ROAST
1 10–12-pound crown roast of pork
Salt and pepper

FOR THE STUFFING
6 tablespoons butter, melted
2 tablespoons olive oil
1 small yellow onion, chopped
1 celery rib including any leaves, chopped

1 teaspoon fennel seeds
1 pound ground pork
Handful chopped fresh parsley leaves
6–8 fresh sage leaves, chopped
Leaves of 2–3 sprigs fresh thyme
Salt and pepper
3 cups fresh corn bread crumbs
1 apple, peeled, cored, and diced

For the roast, preheat the oven to 350°. Put the roast into a large roasting pan. Generously season the meat all over with salt and pepper.

For the stuffing, heat 2 tablespoons of the butter and the oil together in a large skillet over medium heat. Add the onions, celery, and fennel seeds and cook, stirring occasionally, until the vegetables are soft, about 5 minutes. Add the ground pork and cook, breaking the meat up with the back of a spoon, until it is no longer pink, about 5 minutes. Stir in the herbs and generously season with salt and pepper. Transfer to a large bowl. Add the corn bread and apples and toss to combine.

Fill the center of the crown roast with the stuffing and drizzle with the remaining 4 tablespoons melted butter. Roast the crown roast in the oven until the internal temperature of the pork reaches 155°, about 3 hours. Cover the stuffing with a sheet of foil if it begins to get too browned before the meat is finished cooking.

continued

Remove roast from the oven and let it rest for 20 minutes before transferring it to a large warm platter. Pour any of the accumulated juices from the roasting pan over the stuffing to moisten it, if you like, or you can strain the juices into a gravy boat. Carve the roast by slicing between the ribs.

BAKED APPLES WITH SAVORY STUFFING
makes 8–10

Our Crown Roast of Pork with Corn Bread Stuffing is accompanied by these similarly stuffed baked apples. Sausage meat and fresh breadcrumbs can replace the ground pork and corn bread crumbs and taste equally delicious.

4 tablespoons butter
2 tablespoons olive oil
1 small yellow onion, chopped
1 celery rib including any leaves, chopped
1 teaspoon fennel seeds
1 pound ground pork

Handful chopped fresh parsley leaves
6–8 fresh sage leaves, chopped
Leaves from 2–3 fresh thyme sprigs
Salt and pepper
1 cup fresh corn bread crumbs
8–10 apples

Preheat the oven to 350°. Heat 2 tablespoons of the butter and the oil together in a large skillet over medium heat. Add the onions, celery, and fennel seeds and cook, stirring occasionally, until the vegetables are soft, about 5 minutes. Add the ground pork and cook, breaking the meat up with the back of a spoon until it is no longer pink, about 5 minutes. Stir in the herbs and generously season with salt and pepper. Transfer to a large bowl. Add the corn bread and toss to combine.

Cut off the top third of each apple and, using a small spoon, scoop out the center, removing the core, seeds, and just enough of the flesh to make a nice hollow for the stuffing. Divide the stuffing evenly between the apples, packing it into each hollow. Transfer the stuffed apples to a large baking dish. Dot each apple with a small knob of the remaining 2 tablespoons butter.

Bake the apples until the flesh is tender and the stuffing is golden brown, about 1 hour.

PARSNIP PURÉE
serves 6–8

Parsnips have a wonderful affinity with apples and pears. The fruit adds a natural sweetness to the earthy root vegetables. Don't add too much water to the pot when cooking the parsnips—why pour all the flavor down the drain?

3 pounds parsnips, peeled and sliced

2 russet potatoes, peeled and sliced

2 apples or pears, peeled, cored
   and sliced

6 tablespoons butter

Salt and pepper

Put the parsnips, potatoes, apples or pears, butter, ½ cup water, and salt and pepper to taste into a medium, heavy-bottomed pot. Cover and cook over medium heat, stirring from time to time, until everything is very soft, about 40 minutes. Mash or purée the vegetables (don't drain them!) to the consistency that you like—it can be very smooth or quite rustic.

Spoon the parsnips into an ovenproof serving dish, if you like, and keep warm in the oven until you are ready to serve. Drizzle a little melted butter on top.

BÛCHE DE NOËL
serves 8–12

Turn off the phone, turn up the Christmas carols, roll up your sleeves, and give yourself over to making this spectacular traditional Christmas dessert.

FOR THE CHOCOLATE ICING
6 ounces semisweet chocolate
4 tablespoons unsalted butter
⅓ cup heavy cream

FOR THE MERINGUE MUSHROOMS
3 egg whites, at room temperature
Pinch of salt
¼ teaspoon cream of tartar
1 cup granulated sugar
1 teaspoon vanilla extract
1 tablespoon unsweetened cocoa
2–3 tablespoons Chocolate Icing

FOR THE ROULADE
2 tablespoons unsalted butter, at room temperature

8 ounces bittersweet chocolate, chopped
1 cup heavy cream
7 egg whites, at room temperature
2 tablespoons granulated sugar
2 tablespoons dark rum, optional

FOR THE CHOCOLATE FILLING
4 ounces semisweet chocolate
6 tablespoons granulated sugar
3 egg yolks
12 tablespoons unsalted butter, at room temperature

Powdered sugar, for the final dusting of "snow"

For the chocolate icing, melt chocolate and butter together in a heatproof bowl set over a pot of simmering water over medium-low heat, whisking often. Remove bowl from heat and whisk in cream. Set the icing aside, stirring from time to time, until it has thickened but is still spreadable, about 1 hour. Don't refrigerate, it will make the icing too hard to spread.

For the meringue mushrooms, preheat the oven to 225°. Cover a cookie sheet with foil. Put the egg whites into a mixing bowl and beat with an electric mixer on medium-low speed until frothy. Add the salt and cream of tartar and beat on medium speed until very soft peaks form, about 1 minute. Continue beating while adding the sugar, 1 heaping tablespoon at a time, beating for approximately 30 seconds between each addition. Add vanilla and beat on high speed until very stiff peaks form and the sugar has dissolved (rub some of the

continued

whites between your thumb and forefinger to check if the granules have dissolved and the whites are smooth), 10–15 minutes.

Transfer the meringue to a large pastry bag fitted with a ¼-inch plain pastry tip. To make the meringue mushrooms, hold the pastry tip perpendicular to the foil-lined cookie sheet and pipe the meringue into the shapes of mushroom caps and stems of various sizes (caps can be 1–2 inches wide; stems about 1 inch tall) about 1 inch apart from each other. Let the meringue mushrooms rest for 5 minutes, then moisten your fingertip in cold water and smooth out any points left behind on the mushroom caps. Very lightly dust the caps with cocoa. You'll need a dozen or so meringue mushrooms to decorate the bûche de Noël, but don't worry, they'll all get eaten.

Bake the meringues until they are firm to the touch and can easily be peeled off the foil but have not colored (they should remain white), 1–1½ hours. Turn off the oven, prop open the oven door a bit, and leave the meringues in the oven until they are crisp and dry, about 1 hour.

When the meringues are cool, bore a small shallow hole in the center of the underside of each mushroom cap with the tip of a paring knife. Smear the underside of each cap with some chocolate icing, filling the hole as well, and glue a stem into each cap by sticking the tip of the stem into the hole.

continued

For the roulade, preheat the oven to 375°. Line a jelly roll pan with buttered parchment paper cut large enough to hang over the sides of the pan by about 2 inches and set aside.

Put chocolate into a large mixing bowl. Heat the cream in a heavy-bottomed saucepan until hot, then pour over the chocolate and whisk until smooth. Set the chocolate aside and let it cool.

Put the egg whites in a mixing bowl and beat with an electric mixer on medium speed until frothy. Increase speed to medium-high and gradually add sugar, beating constantly. Increase speed to high and beat until peaks are stiff but not dry. Gently fold the whites into the chocolate using a rubber spatula, taking care not to deflate the batter. Spread the batter evenly in the prepared pan and bake until a toothpick inserted into the center comes out clean, about 10 minutes. Set aside to let the cake cool in the pan.

For the chocolate filling, put the chocolate and 2 tablespoons water into a medium heatproof bowl set over a pot of simmering water over medium heat. Stir until the chocolate has melted and the mixture is smooth. Remove the bowl from the heat and let the chocolate cool.

Combine the granulated sugar and 3 tablespoons water in a small saucepan; cover and bring to a boil over medium heat, swirling the pan several times until the sugar has dissolved, about 1 minute. Uncover the pan and let the sugar syrup boil until it reaches the soft ball stage or 236° on a candy thermometer, about 5 minutes more. Meanwhile, beat the egg yolks in a mixing bowl with an electric mixer on high speed until they are thick and pale yellow. Reduce the speed to medium and gradually pour in the hot syrup. Beat constantly until the egg mixture cools to room temperature, about 10 minutes. Beat in the butter, 1 tablespoon at a time, beating thoroughly after each addition. Continue beating the buttercream together until thick and smooth, about 5 minutes all together. Stir in the cooled chocolate and set the filling aside.

To assemble the bûche de Noël, carefully transfer the roulade with the parchment paper to a clean work surface. Sprinkle the surface of the cake with the rum, if using, then spread the chocolate filling evenly over the top

continued

of the cake using an offset spatula or a butter knife. Grab the long edge of the parchment paper, one hand at each end, and gently roll the cake onto itself pulling the paper off as you roll it into a roulade. The cake may crack lengthwise into pieces as you roll, but don't worry, as the filling will keep the roulade in shape and the icing will cover any cracks. Discard the parchment paper. To make two "stumps", diagonally cut a 2-inch length from each end of the roulade and set them aside.

Using two long metal spatulas, carefully transfer the bûche de Noël to a serving platter. Slip a few strips of parchment paper under the edges of the roulade (the strips help keep the platter clean when you ice the cake). Spread the ends (not the cut side) of each stump with some of the chocolate icing, then glue each stump onto the roulade. Spread the icing over the stumps and roulade leaving the spiral ends to look like age rings of the "wooden log". If the icing becomes too firm to spread easily, put the bowl over a pot of gently simmering water until the icing around the edge of the bowl begins to melt. Remove the bowl from the heat and whisk the icing until it is smooth and has the consistency of very very soft butter. Drag the spatula along the icing on the log to imitate tree bark. Remove and discard the paper strips from the platter.

Decorate the bûche de Noël with the meringue mushrooms, then sift powdered sugar over the mushrooms and log to resemble freshly fallen snow.

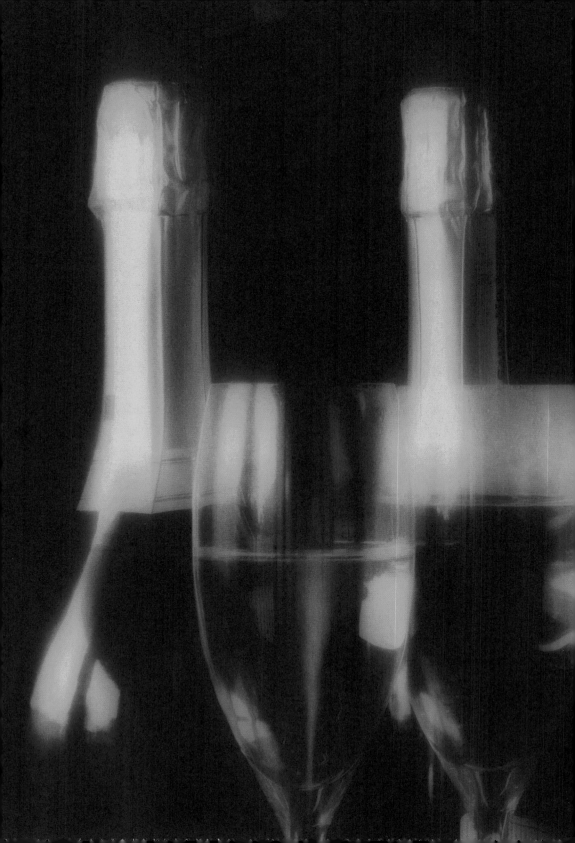

happy new year

ROGER SHERMAN'S BLINI
serves 4

Filmmaker Roger Sherman is married to our dear friend Dorothy Kalins, the renowned editor who thought up and started *Saveur* magazine. They have the most hospitable of homes. Drop by unannounced with a little beluga and Roger might just whip up a batch of his famous blini. Here's how he makes them.

1 cup cottage cheese
¼ cup whole wheat flour
3 eggs

2 tablespoons canola oil, plus more
   for oiling the skillet

Put all the ingredients in a blender. Blend until the batter is smooth.

Use a paper towel to rub a large skillet with a little oil. Heat skillet over medium-high heat. Drop tablespoonfuls of batter into the hot skillet a couple inches apart. Cook until little bubbles form on surface of the blini. Flip blini and cook for less than a minute. Transfer to a platter and top with caviar or salmon eggs.

CHEESE STRAWS
makes about 36

These are also good sprinkled with black pepper, cayenne, or pimentón.

1¼ cups finely grated parmigiano-reggiano
2 sheets puff pastry, defrosted (but not unfolded)

Preheat oven to 375°. Dust a clean work surface with about ¼ cup of the grated cheese. Put 1 unfolded sheet of puff pastry on top of the cheese and dust it with another ¼ cup of cheese. Roll pastry out with a rolling pin into a rectangle about ⅛ inch thick, dusting it with more cheese, if necessary.

Using a sharp knife or a pastry cutter, cut pastry into long ½-inch-wide strips. Twist each strip several times into the shape of a corkscrew and lay them on a parchment paper–lined baking sheet about ½ inch apart. Repeat the rolling out and cutting and twisting process with the remaining sheet of puff pastry and cheese.

Bake the cheese straws until they are puffed and golden, about 10 minutes. Let them cool to room temperature before peeling them off the paper.

COQ AU VIN
serves 6–8

The star of this dish should be a rooster (or *coq*, as the French say). This classic French recipe was most likely built around what-to-do-when-the-rooster-died. This tough but flavorful bird needed long cooking and wine to coax it into tenderness. Today, finding a rooster in a supermarket is unlikely, so rather than using an all-purpose young chicken, look for a capon (a young castrated rooster) or use a large stewing hen. You can make this stew a day or two ahead and gently reheat on top of the stove or in a low oven.

One 6–7-pound capon, stewing hen, or roaster, cut into 10 pieces
8–10 shallots, peeled
2–3 medium carrots, peeled and diced
3–4 cloves garlic
1 branch fresh thyme
2 bay leaves
1½ bottles wine (red or white, either one is fine)

Salt and pepper
2 tablespoons butter
¼ pound thick-sliced bacon, diced
½ pound white mushrooms, quartered lengthwise
1 tablespoon tomato paste
2 tablespoons flour
¼ cup Cognac
2 tablespoons unsweetened cocoa

Put the capon, shallots, carrots, garlic, thyme, bay leaves, and wine into a large bowl to marinate. Cover and refrigerate for 1–2 days.

Reserving the marinade, remove the capon and pat the pieces dry with paper towels. Season the capon with salt and pepper and set aside.

Preheat the oven to 325°. Melt the butter in a large enameled cast iron pot over medium heat. Add the bacon and fry until crisp, about 5 minutes. Drain the bacon on paper towels, leaving the rendered fat in the pot. Add the mushrooms and cook, stirring from time to time, until lightly browned, about 5 minutes. Transfer the mushrooms to a bowl and set aside. (The bacon and mushrooms aren't added to the stew until the very end.)

continued

Increase the heat to medium-high. Working in batches to avoid crowding the pot, add the capon pieces, browning them all over (add a little oil to the pot if needed). Transfer them to a plate as they finish.

Reduce the heat to medium and stir the tomato paste and the flour into the pot. Stir in the cognac, scraping up any browned bits stuck to the bottom of the pot. Stir in the marinade (including the vegetables and aromatics). Add the capon and any accumulated juices from the plate to the pot. The liquid in the pot should just cover the meat; add more wine, or some chicken stock or water, if necessary. Bring to a simmer. Partially cover the pot and transfer to the oven. Cook the stew until the capon is very tender, about 1½ hours.

Remove the capon from the pot with a slotted spoon and set aside. Strain the vegetables over a bowl. Discard the thyme branch. Set vegetables aside. Return the sauce to the pot. Whisk in the cocoa. Simmer the sauce over medium heat until thickened a bit, 10–20 minutes. Taste the sauce and season with salt and pepper.

Return the vegetables, capon, and mushrooms to the pot and warm everything together over low heat. Add the bacon just before serving. Serve with buttered boiled potatoes or noodles, if you like.

WATERCRESS SALAD
serves 6–8

Mash together a minced small clove garlic with a good pinch of salt and some pepper in the bottom of a salad bowl. Stir in the juice of half a lemon. Add 4–6 tablespoons really good extra-virgin olive oil, stirring as you do so. Taste the vinaigrette and adjust the seasoning. Add 1 bunch of chopped scallions to the bowl, stirring them into the vinaigrette. Pile 4 bunches cleaned watercress and the cleaned tender inner leaves of 1 small head bibb lettuce on top of the vinaigrette. Toss the salad just before serving. It wilts quickly.

GRAND MARNIER SOUFFLÉ
serves 2–4

This magnificent dessert requires an audience, even if it's only two. So practice making one or two before you debut your soufflé-making abilities.

4 tablespoons butter, softened
8 tablespoons granulated sugar, plus
  more for dusting
Finely grated rind of 1 orange
3 tablespoons flour, sifted
¾ cup whole milk
4 egg yolks

¼ cup Grand Marnier or other
  orange liqueur
1 teaspoon vanilla extract
5 egg whites, at room temperature
Pinch of salt
Powdered sugar

Set an oven rack in the middle of the oven and preheat oven to 375°. Butter a 4-cup soufflé dish (the soufflé won't rise as tall if using a larger dish) with 1 tablespoon of the butter and dust it with granulated sugar, tapping out any excess. Prepare a collar for the soufflé dish by buttering one side of a long 4-inch-wide strip of parchment paper with 1 tablespoon butter, then dust it with some granulated sugar. Wrap the prepared side of the parchment paper around the outside of the soufflé dish and tie it in place with kitchen string. It should rise above the rim of the dish by about 3 inches. Set the dish aside.

Mix orange rind with 7 tablespoons of the granulated sugar in a heavy saucepan, off the heat. Stir in the flour. Add the milk, stirring until smooth. Bring to a boil over medium heat, stirring constantly, and cook until thick, about 30 seconds.

Remove pan from the heat. Whisk in the egg yolks one at a time, whisking well after each addition. Whisk in remaining 2 tablespoons butter. Put the orange mixture into a large bowl and stir in the liqueur and vanilla.

Beat egg whites and salt together in another large bowl with an electric mixer on medium-low speed until whites are foamy and hold soft peaks. Add the remaining 1 tablespoon of the granulated sugar and beat on high speed until stiff but not dry peaks form. Using a rubber spatula, fold about one-third of the egg whites into the orange mixture to lighten it, then gently fold in the rest. Spoon the soufflé mixture into prepared dish, filling it to ½-inch from rim of the dish.

Bake until soufflé is puffed and browned, about 30 minutes. Dust with powdered sugar and present it immediately. Remove collar; spoon soufflé onto 2–4 plates.

RAMOS FIZZ
makes 2

This traditional New Orleans cocktail is a great hair of the dog if you are nursing a hangover. With all that icy cold milk, it feels downright healthy as it goes down. You may need to seek out a source for the orange-flower water, but do so, because it is vital to the drink's distinctive perfumed taste.

¾ cup whole milk
3 ounces dry gin
1 teaspoon fresh lemon juice
1 teaspoon fresh lime juice

1 teaspoon orange-flower water
1 egg white
2 tablespoons powdered sugar

Put the milk, gin, lemon and lime juices, orange-flower water, egg white, and powdered sugar into a cocktail shaker filled with ice cubes. Cover and shake vigorously. Pour into 2 tall glasses and serve.

BITTER GREENS WITH SWEET GRAPEFRUIT
serves 4

My aunt Peg, who lives in Florida, sends my family a bushel box of Indian River Ruby Red grapefruit every year for Christmas. We're never sure if we'll make it through the whole box. But we juice them, broil them with brown sugar, candy the pinkish rinds, and make this bright salad. By the time winter's over we're down to our last few grapefruit. Keep 'em coming, Aunt Peg. —— MH

1 grapefruit, preferably a pink one
1 tablespoon wine vinegar
6 tablespoons really good extra-
  virgin olive oil

Salt and pepper
6 cups bitter greens

Slice the ends off the grapefruit. Set the grapefruit on one of the cut ends and slice off the rind and white pith, exposing the flesh. Working over a salad bowl to catch any juice, slice between each fruit segment, cutting it away from the membrane and let the segments and juice fall into the bowl.

Squeeze any juice from the spent grapefruit into the bowl. Add vinegar and stir in the olive oil. Season with salt and pepper. Pile salad greens on top. Toss well just before serving.

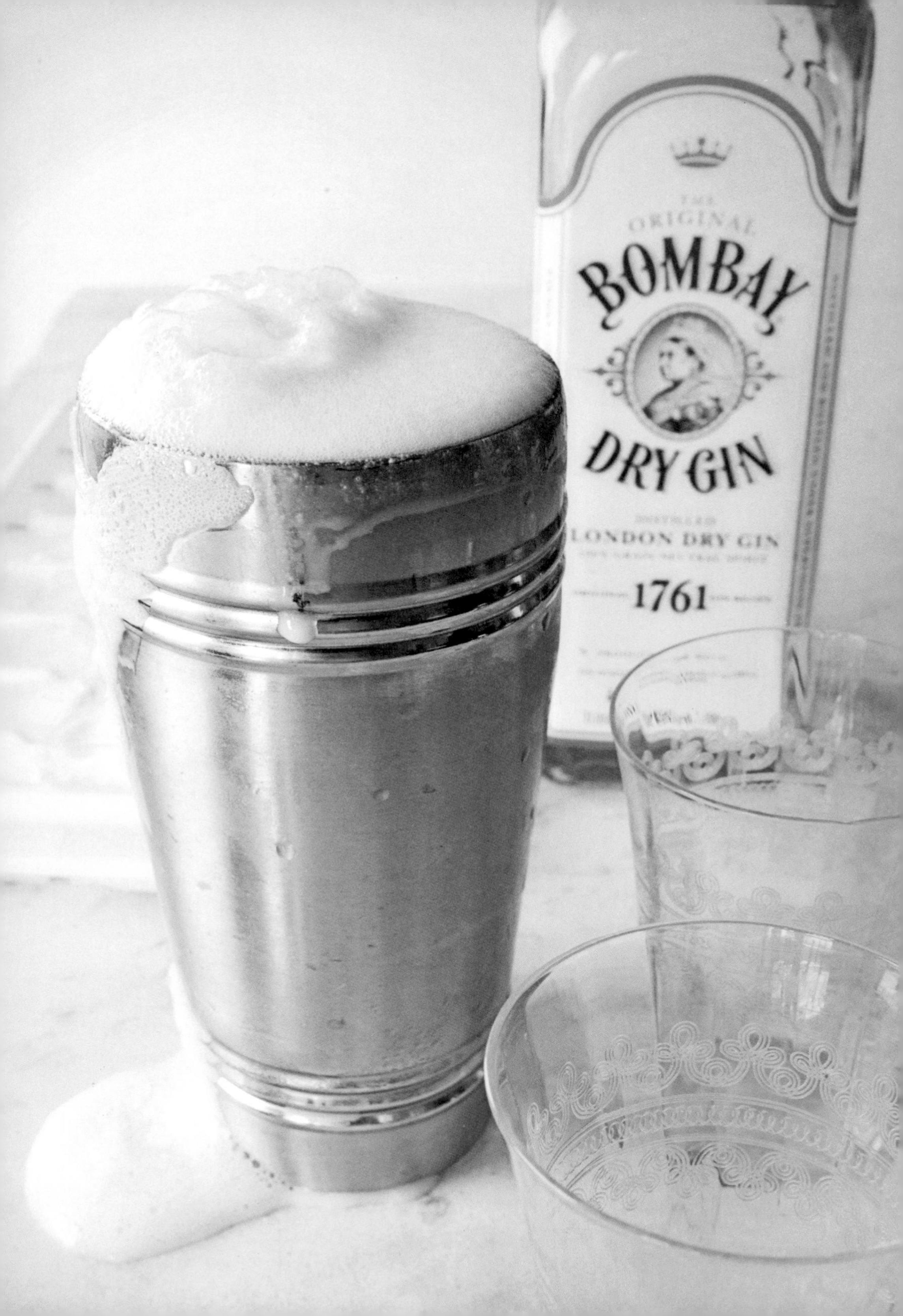
ORIGINAL
BOMBAY
DRY GIN
LONDON DRY GIN
1761

EGGS EN COCOTTE
makes 4

The gentle, even cooking of the eggs in their ramekins in the hot water bath keeps them tender and prevents them from cooking too fast. We make this simple egg and cream dish more or less luxurious depending on the occasion. Sometimes we make it with two eggs, or we'll nestle a couple of spoonfuls of cooked spinach, or some sliced black truffles, or poached shrimp or lobster in the bottom of each ramekin. We also make this dish with pieces of poached chicken. There's something particularly satisfying and ironic about eating the chicken and the egg all in one. Who cares which came first—it's delicious.

4 tablespoons butter, softened

¾ cup heavy cream

½ cup poached chicken or lobster chunks, small peeled raw shrimp, cooked spinach, or a few slices of black truffle

Salt and pepper

4 eggs

Ground nutmeg

Small handful chopped chives, tarragon, parsley, or other tender herbs

Preheat the oven to 400°. Butter four 4-ounce custard cups or deep ramekins with 2 tablespoons of the butter. Add a splash of the heavy cream to each cup and set aside.

Generously season the chicken or other ingredient of your choosing with salt and pepper, then nestle some of it into the bottom of each cup. Crack an egg into each cup. Season each with a little salt and pepper and a pinch of nutmeg. Divide the remaining cream between the cups, carefully pouring it over each egg. The cream should pretty much cover the eggs. Season with a little more salt, pepper, and nutmeg. Top each with a knob of the remaining 2 tablespoons butter.

Set the cups into a deep pan filled halfway with simmering water. Carefully transfer the pan to the oven. Bake the eggs until the cream is bubbling, the tops have browned, and the eggs are barely set (they should tremble when you jiggle the cups), about 10 minutes. The eggs will continue to cook once they've been removed from the water bath.

Remove the cups from the water bath and sprinkle the eggs with chopped herbs. Serve the eggs in their cups with slices of hot buttered toast.

OUR BOOKS

This is the second book of our recipe collections—Canal House Cooking. We'll publish three seasonal volumes a year: Summer, Fall & Holiday, and Winter & Spring, each filled with delicious recipes for you from us. To sign up for a subscription or to buy books, visit thecanalhouse.com.

OUR WEBSITE

Our website, thecanalhouse.com, a companion to this book, offers our readers ways to get the best from supermarkets (what and how to buy, how to store it, cook it, and serve it). We'll tell you why a certain cut of meat works for a particular recipe, which boxes, cans, bottles, or tins are worthwhile; which apples are best for baking; and what to look for when buying olive oil, salt, or butter. We'll also suggest what's worth seeking out from specialty stores or mail-order sources and why. And wait, there's more. We will share our stories, the wines we are drinking, gardening tips, and events; and our favorite books, cooks, and restaurants will all be on our site.

thank you
eat well